MY LIFE
A PATCHWORK

MY LIFE
A PATCHWORK

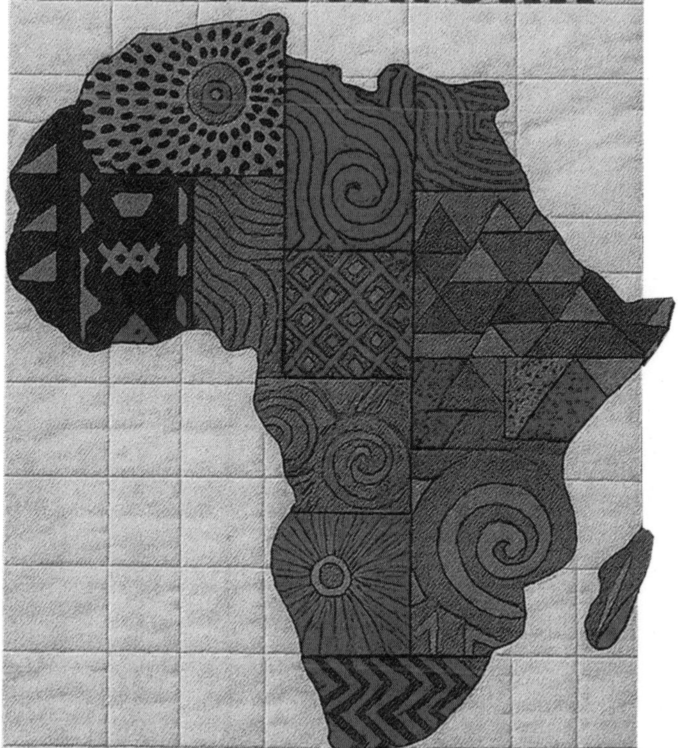

AISHA LOWE

First published in Great Britain in 2025 by
Bannister Publications Ltd
Offices 2A, Market Hall, Chesterfield, Derbyshire, S40 1AR

ISBN: 978-1-916823-28-0
(paperback)

A catalogue record for this book is available from the British Library

Printed and bound in Great Britain by CMP (UK) Ltd

BANNISTER
PUBLICATIONS

This book is dedicated with love to the memory of the five people who brought me up. I am sad they are not here to see this, but I will never forget them: my mother, Mwanaima; my father, Athumani; my uncle, Mzee Zuberi; my adoptive mother, Mama Khadija; and my young sister, Maridhia.

Contents

Introduction

I was born in 1957 in Tanzania, then known as Tanganyika before it became an independent country in 1962. In that same year my parents separated, and my aunt took me to Kenya to live with her. Although I grew up in Kenya, I still maintained strong family connections in Tanzania. At the age of twenty-seven, I moved to England with my husband and four children. At the time, I didn't realise how momentous this change was for me; it marked the beginning of a life I could never have imagined for myself as a child. At twenty-seven I embarked on a life of travel, experiencing different countries and cultures; meeting and making friends with people from many different parts of the world.

I have written something about this in my previous book, *"A Tale for my Children and Grandchildren."*

Responses from family, friends and other readers encouraged me to write this second book. Here, I take my story further, adding more experiences, memories and detail. Taken all together these make up the story of my life and the various contexts in which it has unfolded. But I am not telling my story in strict chronological order, from when I was a child to who I am today. My tale meanders through different landscapes and different times but in an order that is influenced by who I have become and what is important to me now. I believe that when we look back on the past, we do not always do it in a linear way, from past to present. Memories spring up in isolation but still in some way related to each other, and that is the way I see my life when I look back on it. The result is that my life appears to me as something like a patchwork quilt, and I try to capture this in this book. The quilt is made from my experiences, observations and reflections, all seen through my eyes, but I know that how I have seen - and still see - the world has been influenced by other people and places that appear in my story.

There is a pattern in my quilt, a pattern that comes from my choice of which incidents and influences to include and how they are arranged. In my head are lots of bits of coloured cloth. These are the 'happenings' of my life. I will pull them out as they attract my attention (for whatever reasons) and lay them out in front of you. Seen altogether they form the patchwork quilt that is my life. But I - as I was, as I am now and as I now think I was – am the thread holding these bits of cloth together to make the pattern of the life I present. I hope it makes some sense to you and that you enjoy the pattern as it appears in the book.

As I reveal different parts of the quilt you will meet my family. Some of them appear very early on in this story and if I don't introduce them to you right at the beginning, you won't know who I am talking about when I use their names. So, let me briefly introduce us all here. You may find out more about each and all of us as I present my quilt to you.

I am Aisha and my husband is John. We have four children, all now grown up. Our first child is a daughter, Tuni, who is married to Simon and they have two children, Savannah and Zain. Following Tuni there is Mani and his three children, Aaliyah, Will and Damien. His wife is Umi. Our second daughter, Farida, is married to Jeremy, and is mother to Layla, Ezra and Sahara. Our fourth child and second son is Nurudin and his partner Gemma and her daughter Leah.

Chapter 1

Growing up in East Africa

People from the rest of the world often see Africa in terms of its wildlife, they think of the famous national parks, such as Serengeti or Kruger. Certainly, in England, I have found that the most people ever see of Tanzania are the numerous wildlife films on TV. These are beautiful to look at and make me very proud, but where are the people? Is Tanzania a country empty of human beings? One of the things I want to do in this book is explain that there is more to East Africa than wild animals and magnificent scenery. I hope I can show that the people of East Africa are worthy of interest too.

It is unfortunate that so much of the wildlife in Tanzania — and elsewhere in East Africa — is under threat. Most people are aware that illegal poaching is one of the main threats to wildlife, but there is much more to it than that. It is a complex issue that involves the way the people of the country interact with the wildlife they live alongside. If we knew more about the livelihoods of ordinary Tanzanians, we might come to appreciate the issue from their point of view. The people of Tanzania do care about wild animals, but they are also poor, and poaching is often the only means available to them to support themselves and their families. That said, most people do not engage in actual poaching, nor do they support it. More of a concern for the people I know — and from my own experience — is the danger that wildlife can present to their farms and that crops that are their main source of livelihood. When I was a child (a little while ago now), one of the tasks that I and the other children were given to do was to chase the baboons who invaded our maize crop and "shared" the harvest. Believe me, baboons may look cute on TV, but they can be very dangerous, especially the male leaders of the troop. Even as I write this, my cousins are telling me of elephants that are invading their farms. When elephants come into a farm, they tend to clear just about everything edible. Elephants are really dangerous animals that cannot be chased away by small children, or adults. Try to chase an elephant and you are in danger of being trampled to death.

So, while being well aware of the amazing wildlife we have in my home country, I want in my book to balance the common image of East Africa as a land of beautiful scenery (which it is) and spectacular wild animals (which they are) by focusing on the lives of ordinary people like myself and my family. We have a rich culture that few people are aware of, except in terms of the exotic. There is a lot more to the people of East Africa than the "tribal dance" or the witch doctor. Like people all over the world, we go about our daily business in the environment in which we find ourselves. What may look exotic or strange to you is for us, just "life."

I spent my childhood partly in Kenya and partly in Tanzania. This is not like living in, say, England and France. The people on either side of the Kenya/Tanzania border share a common language, *Kiswahili*. They eat similar food and have almost identical cultures. This is because the border between the two countries was not arrived at through war, but was arbitrarily imposed, drawn on a map by foreign colonialists — the English in Kenya and the Germans in Tanganyika — and had no relation to national or cultural identity. When I was a child, local people moved freely between the two countries — going to the markets, visiting friends and family, or even going to school. Local people do still cross the border using "unofficial" routes (which usually involves moving on foot, or by canoe). The "official" border is just like that separating any two countries, with border posts, customs officials who demand identity documents and search through baggage. Nevertheless, there are many families — such as my own — whose members live on both sides of the border, and people and goods regularly move between the two, especially local produce that is taken to be sold in the markets.

I spent the first five years of my life living with my parents in a small village in north-eastern Tanzania. My village was then in the British Protectorate of Tanganyika. Shortly after I moved to Kenya, which was still a British colony, Tanganyika gained its independence, eventually becoming known as the Republic of Tanzania. Throughout all these changes, life in my birth village of Usangi, its people and their language and culture, continued as it always had done.

My parents lived high up in the Pare Mountains. Despite the common perception of Africa as being always hot and dry, believe me, it can be very cold up on those hills. In the cold season the fire in our house was constantly kept alight — or at least the embers kept glowing — to keep us from freezing. When I was still very young, my parents' marriage broke up, and I was eventually taken to Kenya to live with my aunt Khadija, my father's half-sister. I have written about this in more detail in my first book, "A *Tale for my Children and Grandchildren,*" so I will not repeat the story here. In this book, I turn my attention to my experiences of life in the various parts of the world in which I have lived and travelled, and what I have learned from them. I don't pretend to be a cultural anthropologist, and so the observations, understanding and experiences that I relate are from my own personal viewpoint.

Although I did not grow up in Tanzania, I remember much about it from my childhood years, and I visit the country regularly, as I still have family living there. Tanzania has always been poorer than Kenya, and still is, although both countries have their wealthy elites. So, my aunt Khadija and her husband, Mzee Zuberi, were persuaded to move to Kenya because it seemed to offer more opportunities for a better life.

Tourists may be familiar with the area in which I grew up because it is home to Mount Kilimanjaro, the highest mountain in Africa. I grew up against the backdrop of this beautiful mountain, and have seen it in all the different seasons. At the time I didn't realise that I would be among the last of those people fortunate to see it in its full glory. Sadly, Kilimanjaro is no longer what it was, for one simple reason: climate change. Young people in Tanzania and Kenya will never see it as I did in the 1970s. I clearly recall standing outside my younger sister's house in Kisangara, in the Pare hills, and seeing Kilimanjaro covered in snow, from the tops of its two distinctive peaks right down to the saddle between them. It is a sight rarely, if ever, witnessed today.

Climate change is not the only way in which the outside world has affected the Africa that was my first home. There is a widely told story in East Africa regarding the location of Mount Kilimanjaro. I have already mentioned Tanzania's change of name at independence. When Tanganyika, as it was then called, was a German colony, the Kaiser, whose name was Wilhelm, was the nephew of the British Queen, Victoria. When civil servants from Britain and Germany were negotiating the border between Kenya and Tanganyika, Wilhelm asked his aunt to draw the boundary so that Mount Kilimanjaro was included in "his" colony rather than "hers." Kaiser Wilhelm argued that Victoria already had snow-covered Mount Kenya in her colony, and he wanted one just as spectacular for himself. Naturally, the people actually living in the area weren't consulted. As with climate change, we just had to accept it.

At the age I was then, I wasn't particularly interested in the snows of Kilimanjaro. I never climbed the mountain; nobody back then thought of doing so. By the time I left Africa, I had never seen snow up close, let alone touched it. We did have a name for it — *theluji* in *Kiswahili,* but had no idea what it was like. We had never seen ice in a refrigerator, nor even frost. I didn't have any experience of the "white stuff" until 1984, when I arrived in England with my husband, John, and our four children, not long before Christmas. We went to stay with my parents-in-law, and woke up the day after our arrival, still tired after a long flight from Kenya via Sudan, to find the world outside the windows blanketed in white. I hadn't even realised that snow wasn't only to be found on mountains, but in the streets and covering the houses. The children had no idea what it was. Neither had they experienced cold. Coastal Kenya is humid, generally hot, or very hot, and slightly cooler when it rains. They had to get used to wearing several layers of clothes, to having to put on coats, gloves, woolly hats, whenever they went outside. They had never worn so many clothes in their lives!

That day, in 1984, the snow covered everything, and was still falling. When I had seen distant *theluji* on Mount Kilimanjaro I had assumed it was just there, it never occurred to me that it fell from the sky, as rain does. It looked to me like white ash falling from the sky. In his excitement, our son Mani rushed outside in his bare feet, just as he was used to doing back home in Kenya, but ran back into the house the moment he realised his mistake. It was an important early lesson for him! He and the other children quickly learned about cold and that they could no longer wear just the flip-flops that they were used to. They had to learn about coats, woolly hats, gloves and wellies. I, too, went outside and picked up snow with my bare hands for the first time in my life. I learned that cold can really bite.

But that is another part of the patchwork, one I'll return to later. For now, let me take you back to East Africa and the way outsiders see it and its people. It's a sad fact that you can't talk about Africa's amazing wildlife without the topic of poaching coming up. It is still prevalent in both Kenya and Tanzania. Elephants are killed for their tusks, rhinos for their horns; lions, leopards, zebras, giraffes and many other beautiful animals are massacred for their skins. The illegal international trade in wildlife products has made big money for those involved. There is another kind of poaching that is less talked about but has been part of Africans' way of life forever. This is hunting for food. It is not about making money; it is about poor people feeding themselves and their families in hard times, such as during droughts. My father had a bow and arrows that he used to hunt small animals for the pot. The bow and arrows are still hanging in my father's house in Usangi, though no one uses them anymore. In fact, we have a similar bow and arrows, made in the traditional way, hanging in our house in Derbyshire. These are a memento, a symbol of my heritage; rest assured, they are not used to hunt the Derbyshire wildlife!

Fortunately, people are more aware of the negative consequences of "big" poaching — for the environment, for the national economy and for people themselves. Stamping out this type of poaching needs a level of resources and organisation that is simply beyond what the ordinary people can manage. Corruption is still a big factor in the continuation of the illegal trade in wildlife products. Senior figures in business and even the government are said to be behind it, and if that is the case, it will be hard to stop it from happening. The authorities discourage ordinary people from poaching, but they take the risk because they simply bribe their way out of punishment. Corruption in East Africa doesn't only involve those in powerful positions, it permeates the whole society. In the absence of a fairly paid police force, it is often the only way to "get things done." It is called *chai* in *Kiswahili,* meaning "tea," a euphemism for money paid to look the other way.

Let me give you one example from my own experience of the use of *chai*. I was travelling from my home village of Usangi to Moshi in a mini-bus — known as *matatu* in *Kiswahili* — overloaded with far too many passengers. Besides being hot and uncomfortable, this overloading is dangerous and also illegal. Halfway through our journey, a traffic policeman ordered the driver to stop. He was pulled aside while the policeman checked the tyres, which were slightly worn. He and the driver then held a muttered discussion, and I saw the driver hand over something which could only have been money. The policeman pocketed his *chai,* and waved him off. None of the other passengers showed the slightest surprise at this very obvious act of bribery. Nor was I surprised, because my younger sister had told me many stories of similar occurrences. At that time she ran a small business transporting various products to Dar-es-Salaam. Her lorries were regularly stopped and searched, but all she had to do was give the policeman some *chai,* and she could continue her journey. By the end of his shift, the policeman would have drunk enough "tea" to give himself a decent monthly wage.

This is one of the major factors behind the corruption in Tanzania and Kenya. The police are badly paid, and rely on *chai* to support their families. This is borne out by a member of my family who is a police officer. He himself does not take bribes because he has strong religious beliefs, even though his salary is just as meagre as his fellow officers'. He is also fortunate in that he owns quite a substantial area of cultivatable land, on which they grow their own food, and have enough left over to sell. It is very common for people in wage-earning employment to also have land, growing food or small-scale cash crops. The possession of one's own piece of land is very important to Africans. In fact, when John and I told my family that we were intending to get married, the fact that John had no land caused my family a great deal of concern. "If you have no land," people asked, "where will you live? Where will you build a house for your wife? Where will you grow food?" People with no land, such as the Maasai, who are nomadic pastoralists, are looked down upon by the *Wapare* - people from the Pare hills, where I come from.

A VISIT TO SERENGETI NATIONAL PARK

The most well-known of all the national parks in East Africa is the Serengeti. You may have seen it in one of the many wildlife films on TV. It may seem odd to you, then, that although I lived in East Africa, I had never even thought of visiting the Serengeti. It was a long way from my home, a difficult and expensive trip on public transport, and, anyway, there was always work to be done at home. It wasn't until 2011, when Farida and Jeremy had one of their three wedding ceremonies at my sister's place in Kisangara (the other two were in London and the south of France), that the opportunity finally arose. Almost the whole family came along — Farida and Jeremy, Tuni, Simon and their daughter Savannah. Tuni was pregnant with Zain at the time, and she found the bumpy roads uncomfortable, so her cousin Mariam gave her a *lesso* which she tied around her belly for support. More about the versatile *lesso* later!

The journey, in a four-wheel-drive vehicle, took a lot longer than I had expected. My family were looking forward to seeing all the different animals and birds in real life, rather than on the screen. We saw lions, antelopes, cheetahs, giraffes, zebras, baboons, buffaloes and many more, not forgetting the many-coloured lizards and the snakes. Some of the snakes were venomous, but we weren't about to get close enough to find out. We Africans tend to treat all snakes as potentially dangerous. It's safer that way.

One of my favourite animals — perhaps the most favourite — is the giraffe. I like the way they spread their legs to drink, and the beautiful colours and patterns of their hides. I had often seen them on the road from my home to Mombasa, but until this trip, I hadn't realised that there is more than one type of giraffe. The Masai giraffe has darker patches separated by irregular, light brown lines all the way down to the bottom of their legs, while the reticulated giraffe has lighter, brown-orange patches separated by thick, bright white lines. They all carry their long necks so elegantly, as if they are going to say, 'Look how beautiful I am'. Zebras are another favourite of mine, again because of their patterned hides. When you think of a zebra, you picture their black and white stripes, but in the Serengeti and Tsavo National Parks they often look red, or black-and-white-and-red. This is because of the red soil on the plains of East Africa, where even the elephants can look red (pink elephants?). Unlike many of the other animals, the zebra isn't aggressive. Watching a herd of zebra can be very relaxing, you know you are safe even close to — unlike the lions, and especially the buffaloes, which are very bad-tempered.

In the early days of our relationship, John and I had a couple of frightening encounters with both buffaloes and elephants. On one occasion we were driving through Tsavo National Park in John's not very reliable old car, when we came across a family of elephants (red ones!). Among them were some calves. Not wishing to disturb them, we switched off the engine and sat to watch. At first, the elephants didn't seem concerned about us, then one of the larger females in the group decided it was time we left, and she began moving towards us. We knew that an angry elephant can easily tip a car over, crushing it and its occupants, so we decided it was time to leave. The car, however, had other ideas, and it refused to start. John kept turning the key in the ignition, again and again, but the car just would not start. Meanwhile, the elephant was picking up speed and getting ever closer. At the very last moment, the car coughed and started, and we shot away in a cloud of red dust. To say we were relieved would be an understatement. Zebras don't do that!

DON'T FORGET THE BIRDS

People tend to visit national parks to see the "big five," and they ignore the incredible variety of birds that can be seen — and not just in the parks either, but across the whole of East Africa. I am told that it is one of great bird-watching sites of the world. Along with the rest of the people I grew up with, however, I took little interest in the spectacular bird life all around me. When John and his brother Nick visited my family in the village of Eldoro and, with binoculars around their necks, went off to look at birds, the local people thought they were crazy. Had they no work to do? I must admit that I only came to share his interest in birds much later in our married life. Nevertheless, there were some birds around the village that were hard to ignore.

One of my favourites are the weaver birds, flocks of which are to be seen near most villages. The chattering of these birds was a constant accompaniment to life in the village. These brightly-coloured yellow, black and grey birds get their name from the nests which they weave into cones and hang from the very ends of the long branches of the acacia trees to protect the eggs from rodents or snakes. They use their beaks like sewing needles, threading long thin strands of grass, leaving a hole at the bottom for getting in and out.

The village people disliked them because they ate the seeds of the maize crops. Some farmers trapped them to eat. My uncle, Mzee Zuberi, once brought my aunt Khadija a number of weaver birds he had killed in this way. She cooked them and we all ate them for supper. It turned out there was hardly any flesh on them, and we never ate them again. I have since come to enjoy watching wild birds, and would be very reluctant to eat any. Back when I was a child, living in the village of Kitoghoto, my family and I often ate pigeons. They had more meat than the weaver birds. Now I have learned more about wild birds and their habits, and have come to understand their position in the living world. In the end, we are all interdependent creatures and should live together peaceably.

Another particularly favourite bird of mine is the Ground Hornbill. I first saw these large, beautiful birds when I went to live with my aunt Khadija in the village of Kitoghoto. The villagers believe that sighting one of these birds is a good omen. They feed on insects, snakes and small birds. They lay their eggs in holes in the trees. While the female sits on the eggs, the male forages for food which he brings back to the female. Once the female has laid her eggs, the male bird seals the nest up with mud, leaving just a small hole through which to feed the female, thus protecting them from predators. The female lays three eggs, but once the chicks are hatched, will only feed one, letting the other two die. I guess it is easier to bring up one offspring than three! When the chick is fully-fledged and ready to fly, the mother breaks open the mud and they emerge from the nest. It is fortunate that people respect this bird because they spend most of their time on the ground, and would provide an easy meal. I have been told that if they are left alone, they can live for up to thirty years.

We continued our journey to the Serengeti, stopping every so often to take pictures of the green hills and valleys. The landscape was breathtaking, with birds flying above us against the endless blue sky. Amid all the grandeur, we were able to forget for a time all the problems of the world. Talking of views reminds me of our grandson Ezra, Farida and Jeremy's son. When Ezra was only three years old, we visited Farida and her family in Somerset. While we were there, we all went to Glastonbury Tor. We were determined to climb it, although it really was a bit too much for a three-year-old. We kept telling him that when he got to the top, he would see a beautiful view. This seemed to help him keep going. When we eventually made it to the top, we told him how well he'd done, and how strong he was. "But where's the view?" he asked, puzzled. John tried to explain, saying that a view is everything you can see in front of you. Ezra was silent for a moment, and then he said, "Is that cow down there a view?" Ezra had obviously expected a "view" to be a particular thing, and it was hard for him to comprehend that a view is just everything you see in front of you. Maybe that is how children learn a language.

When we arrived at the Serengeti National Park, we parked our car in front of the office, where we had to pay an entrance fee. Non-residents — Simon, Jeremy and Farida — were expected to pay a lot more than the citizens. I managed to get away with paying the residents' fee, even though I was strictly speaking now a foreigner. I asked Mariam, my sister's daughter, to get tickets for me and Tuni, in case they asked to see our passports, but also because I knew that if they heard me speaking *Kiswahili* they would immediately know that my accent was not local. I was hoping the park officials would consider me to be a Tanzanian from the colour of my skin. Was I, too, being corrupt?

After getting our tickets, we had to leave our own car at the park's office, and were driven around the park by a ranger. This was good for us because he knew the park well, he knew what visitors wanted to see and where to find it. He drove slowly and pointed out the various animals and birds — buffaloes, giraffes, ostriches and many others. We even got close to a pride of lions dozing in the sunshine, who didn't look at all dangerous. How different from the fearful animals of my childhood, where people dreaded lions, making sure to keep doors well secured after nightfall. Having spent most of my life in Kenya, I was familiar with most of the animals we saw in the Serengeti. My youngest son and my grandchildren, however, had only seen them on TV, and seeing them "for real," in their natural habitat was thrilling. They talked about the Serengeti for a long time after they got home.

But now, let's talk about the people living in this area. As I said at the beginning, people outside Africa know a lot about the wildlife from TV but much less about the people.

TWO TRIBES

The villages of my people, the *Wapare,* are nestle in the green, rolling hills and valleys of eastern Tanzania beneath "our mountain," Kilimanjaro. Even if we now live somewhere else, as so often happens these days, we still think of it as "our" place. In fact there are two peoples, or tribes, living next to each other in this region — the *Wapare* and the *Wagweno*. The two tribes have a lot in common: they grow the same crops — maize, yams, sweet potatoes, cassava, coffee and bananas, kidney beans, pawpaw, jackfruits and so on — although they might cook them slightly differently. Each tribe speaks its own mother tongue — *Kipare* and *Kigweno* respectively — but they can communicate with each other in *Kiswahili,* and some members of each tribe can speak the language of the other. We live close to each other and so interact in many ways.

The *Wapare* villages are scattered over the Pare Mountains and on the plains nearby. My parents lived in the small village of Usangi, quite high up in the mountains. I was born there, and the first language I learned was *Kipare,* the language of my parents, family and neighbours. There were people in the village who were not *Wapare,* and from them I learned to speak *Kiswahili,* which is the lingua franca of Tanzania and other East African countries. A knowledge of *Kiswahili* is essential if you want to speak to the local people. Like most people in East Africa, I grew up bilingual, and now I am at least trilingual. In fact, many people there speak more than just two languages; one of my relatives who works at a national radio station speaks nine!

The northern part of the Pare Mountains is known as Ugweno, where the *Wagweno* people live, whose mother tongue is *Kigweno*. Ugweno is very hilly. Water from the hills collects in the valleys during the rainy season, which enables people to grow crops there. The Ugweno hills are higher than those around Usangi. Some of them can be seen from as far away as the Kenyan border. I could easily see them from the village in Kenya where I lived after leaving Usangi. As I grew up they were a constant reminder to me of my birthplace. Like most young children, I didn't appreciate the beauty of the Pare and Ugweno Mountains; they were just there, what I saw every day. I suppose we all get used to where we live, and forget to pay attention to our surroundings. Now I have left, I am very fond of these mountains and always look forward to seeing them whenever I visit, which I do once a year.

The *Wapare* people are very nice and friendly (but I would say that, wouldn't I!) Like everywhere, you find people who like to gossip. Some, too, are jealous of people who are more successful or wealthy. I think much of the gossip and back-biting happens because women socialise with each other, and interaction with men is strongly discouraged. The *Wagweno* people, on the other hand, are easy to get on with, and are always willing go out of their way to help others. When I was living in Kenya, I had a friend from Ugweno whom I became close friends with. She and her family eventually moved back to Tanzania to be near her parents. Sadly, she and her husband passed away a few years ago. I miss her very much, but I remain in contact with her children, who are still in Tanzania.

Other Tribes in my Area

In north-eastern Tanzania, close to the *Wapare*, are the *Wachagga* people, who live on the slopes of Mount Kilimanjaro and on the eastern side of Mount Meru, a bit further to the west. The Chagga people are very lucky because the soil around Kilimanjaro is volcanic in origin, black and very fertile — known as "black cotton soil." It is also very clayey when it is wet. It clings to the soles of your feet, making them heavy, and you feel yourself growing taller as you walk. This good fertile soil enables the *Wachagga* to grow many different kinds of crops, including yams, beans, maize, bananas, oranges, lemons, guavas, avocados, cassava and coffee. They export their coffee globally, and "Grade A Chagga" is considered to be one of the best coffees available. The *Wapare,* too, grow coffee, but not for export.

The *Wachagga* speak *Kichagga,* along with *Kiswahili,* like just about everyone else in Tanzania. They are ethnically related to the *Wapare,* although some *Wapare* refuse to accept this, because they regard the *Wachagga* as thieves. I remember in my teenage years accompanying my aunt Khadija to the market, held every Wednesday and Saturday in Taveta town, which is almost on the border between Kenya and Tanzania. Many *Wachagga* people would cross the border into Kenya to sell their products — second-hand clothes, bead necklaces, hand-made woven baskets, avocados, oranges, yams, live chickens, and slippers made from old tyres for men and women — and more.

Taveta market is held on a big stretch of empty ground with enough space for the many people who come from miles around, even across the border, to sell their wares. It is open, with few trees to give shade, so the vendors try to get there early in the morning, to occupy whatever shade there is. So the buyers get up early too, hoping to buy the produce while it is still fresh. And believe me when it gets hot there, it gets really hot, so in Eldoro anyone intending to go to the market, either to buy or to sell, they will be up as soon as they hear the Imam in the mosque calling people to pray. At five in the morning it is still dark and a bit spooky, so people often travel in groups. When I was young, we all walked the ten kilometres to Taveta town together, carrying the goods we wanted to sell, or empty sacks or baskets if we were going to buy. Nowadays, people use minibuses or '*matatu*', and if you are in a hurry, or don't have much to carry, you can take a motorbike, which is cheaper.

By the time we arrived after our long walk, the market was already quite busy. You would look for people displaying similar products to yours. After a while, the market had organised itself — without anyone directing it — into different sectors: one selling bananas, another with baskets, and slightly apart from these, an area for livestock. Once you had found your space, you swept it clear of litter. There were no litter bins and we tended to throw things just anywhere, except close to the houses — chewed sugarcane, banana skins, empty soda bottles, sweet wrappers and the like. Having tidied your space, you then set out your produce on woven grass mats, sacks or *lessos*, making them look appealing to potential buyers. Occasionally, all your efforts would be spoiled when a dust devil, or *kimbunga* in *Kiswahili*, blew in. This miniature whirlwind would sweep across open dusty areas like the marketplace like a miniature tornado made of red dust. They are unpredictable and can be quite violent — sometimes even strong enough to tear a corrugated iron roof off a house. The usual effect, though, is to blow clothes and other items into the air, covering everything in dust. If a *kimbunga* hits the marketplace, you have to clean up your goods with your *lesso*, and set them out all over again.

Something many white people find surprising is that we Africans tend to feel the sun's direct heat more than those with lighter skins. It is true that we don't burn, but our dark skin absorbs the heat. For this reason, you see African women — especially the older ones — always with a headscarf, while the men wear a *kofia*, or hat. Although Taveta can be very hot, it tends to be a dry heat, rather than the humidity of the coastal areas. The humidity makes you sweaty, sticky and uncomfortable, but the local culture demands that women, in particular, must cover themselves almost from head to toe, making the heat even harder to bear.

On the margins of Taveta market were small shops mostly owned by Indians, selling clothes, shoes, food, cooking oil, paraffin, sugar, tea and other manufactured goods. The reasons for the predominance of Indian-owned shops in Kenyan towns are complex and historical and I won't go into them here. Suffice it to say that these shop owners developed a reputation for mistreating Africans (whether merited or not is still discussed to this day). Certainly, some Africans resented their commercial dominance which they thought made it harder for them to open up their own businesses. Although there was no official apartheid in colonial Africa, the different groups were not encouraged to mix, and after Independence, many Indians sold up and left the country. My father was a tailor, who also had a small general shop in the village of Mata, some way from Taveta. The Indian shops in Taveta were necessary for him, being a source of wholesale items that could not be bought in the market, such as sugar, salt, cooking oil, biscuits, sweets, loose tea, paraffin and so on. So, he would cycle into Taveta every market day to do the shopping for both his home and his store. Whenever I went to the market, I would look out for him on his bicycle. I had been living away from my parents since the age of five, and I missed them very much, so I was always overjoyed to see him. He always gave me ten Kenya shillings "pocket money," which was a lot back then, and I made sure to make it last until the next time I went to market and saw him again. I still miss him very much, and it has nothing to do with his ten shillings!

The market was a meeting place for people from many different tribes, including the *Wakikuyu* and the *Wakamba*, from the highlands of central Kenya; the *Waluhya* and the *Wajaluo* from the far west near Lake Victoria, as well as the people from nearby — the *Wapare* and the *Wachagga*, originally from Tanzania, the *Wataita* from Kenya, and then there were the "true" locals, the *Wataveta*. Thus, as I walked around the market place, I could hear many of the different languages of East Africa. Although I knew odd words from many of these languages, *Kiswahili* was common to all, allowing us to communicate with each other, wherever we came from. We also shared other things in common: we ate similar foods, wore similar clothes, and there were unspoken shared rules about how we should behave and interact.

The market was only a few hundred yards from the Kenya/Tanzania border with people crossing it in both directions, especially on market days. You could get a bus from there to Mombasa, Nairobi in one direction and into

Tanzania in the other. The different bus companies competed for customers, using young boys who, for a tip of about five Kenya shillings, would tout for customers. Anyone wishing to travel to Mombasa, for example, would listen out for those boys touting loudly for the Mombasa buses along with any discount, or other incentive they were offering. The bus would only set off once it was full, and only then would the boys get their five shillings.

As I have said, for some reason people believed that all *Wachagga* were thieves. You often heard somebody yelling that their produce or money had been stolen. Whenever this happened, the people accused were always *Wachagga*. I suspect that people were jealous of the *Wachagga*, who were considered to be better off than people from the other tribes. Certainly, I never found them to be more likely to thieve than any other tribe. I had a Chagga friend who was married to an uncle of mine — my mother's brother — and I got on very well with her. Whenever I visited them, she and her family always made me very welcome. It seems to be common practice for members of one tribe to look down on their neighbours — the closer they are to one another, the greater the resentment. This seems to be a habit wherever I go. I suppose that this "othering" helps to give people of the same tribe a sense of unity.

Another group who were regarded with suspicion were the *Makonde*. At that time I knew little about them, but my aunt sometimes used to point to a group of people – who looked to me no different from anyone else – and tell me they are *Makonde*. These people were originally from Mozambique, and had migrated to Tanzania, and onwards to Kenya, in search of a better life. They are well-known for their unique style of wood carving. I first heard of the *Makonde* in the 1960s when I was still in primary school. At that time, according to aunt Khadija, they were reputed to be cannibals. At the end of market day, my aunt Khadija would say, "We need to leave early and head home before it's dark because the *Makonde* might catch us, and they'll kill us and eat us." I was so scared when she told me that we might be killed, cooked and eaten. Apparently, according to some people in Kitoghoto village, who were told by someone who claimed to 'know' about the habits of the *Makonde,* they considered the tastiest part of a human being to be the feet. Some people were so scared of the *Makonde* "cannibals" that they arranged to travel to and from the market in groups. As a child, I of course believed this story. After all, my elders were my only source of information about the world. Now, I feel sorry for the *Makonde,* who had fled hardship in Mozambique only to be treated with suspicion and even hatred in the country where they had sought refuge. It is a familiar story.

Nowadays, all I hear about the *Makonde* is how good they are at wood-carving, but nothing about cannibalism. They are welcomed and recognised as valued Kenyan citizens. Has the world grown wiser? Sadly, there is enough in the news these days to make me think it hasn't.

Marriages

When I was growing up, the *Wapare* people in Usangi tended to marry someone from the same tribe as themselves, perhaps because they shared the same language and culture, but maybe simply because most people they would meet in their everyday lives would be *Wapare*. In the 1960s, when Aunt Khadija and I had moved just across the border to Kenya, there were people of two tribes living in our village, Kitoghoto. They were the *Wapare* and the *Wakamba,* who had different languages and cultures, and lived on opposite sides of the village. There was no intermarrying amongst them. I came to realise, much later, that this was not just a result of linguistic and cultural differences. Some of the *Wapare* looked down on the *Wakamba,* calling them uneducated and slovenly. *Wapare* parents actively discouraged their sons and daughters from marrying *Wakamba* and this prejudice was passed on to younger people. I can attest to this from my own experience when, as a teenager, I admired a young *Mkamba* man. But I immediately suppressed any feelings towards him because I had been brought up to believe he was beneath me. I am now ashamed that I reacted that way.

I am delighted to say that things have changed quite a lot in recent years and marriages between people from different tribes have become more common. Members of my own extended family have married into different tribes, including even the *Wakamba*! One of my best friends and classmates, a *Mpare,* married a *Mkamba* man. Some — although not all — of the people in her village, including members of her family, privately expressed doubts about the wisdom of this marriage. She went ahead regardless, and they have lived happily together for many years, and have several children. Unfortunately some of us Africans do tend to judge people by where they come from and not on what they are like as individuals. Some of my own family were against my marrying John, although this was more to do with religion than tribe (or skin colour), and the people in my family who mattered most to me supported us. Perhaps I am being too hard on my fellow Africans. You find opposition to marriage between people of different 'backgrounds' in all societies. It happens in the UK, even among the elite.

To me, the *Wakamba* seem extremely hard-working, especially the women — then again, just about all African women work very hard; tilling the land, taking care of children and the men, and so on. Generally, women in Africa are expected to take on considerably more responsibilities than men. Both the *Wakamba* and the *Wapare* women carry their babies strapped on their backs, while at the same time they will be carrying heavy loads on their heads — bundles of firewood, baskets of maize, bunches of bananas, buckets of water, and so on. Men consider this sort of task to be "women's work", menial and beneath their dignity. This is part of the accepted culture, passed down through the generations, making it difficult for them to see that there might be a different way to behave. My aunt told me that when I got married, I must make sure to serve my husband his food first, and give him a bigger portion. It is not only men who pass on these norms; women, too, consider certain jobs their particular responsibility. A woman cousin of mine could hardly believe it when she saw John cooking for us both. She told me I was very lucky, while her husband's response was that cooking is a wife's job.

John could hardly believe his eyes one day, when he saw a *Kamba* lady with her baby on her back while carrying a bundle of firewood on her head, and her husband walked behind, shading himself from the sun with an umbrella. This is perfectly normal among many African peoples. It is tough for women, but many husbands don't seem to appreciate their labours. A lot of men seem to think they own their wives — they are nothing but chattels. Maybe this is because they pay dowry to the family of the woman they wish to marry, which makes them think they have the right to tell them what to do — they have literally bought her! Sometimes women will feel they are like donkeys, but they also think it is their duty. They have been brought up to take care of the household. I have rarely seen an African man doing the housework if the wife is around, unless the wife is sick. All the work of the kitchen, cooking for the family, as well as collecting firewood, milking the cows, pounding maize and winnowing, sweeping the house and compound, washing the family's clothes (I could go on and on) are considered women's jobs. My impression is that women in Africa tend to age faster than men — I guess you can understand why.

Many women, certainly in Kenya and Tanzania, seem to learn to regard themselves as second-class citizens. The man is the head of the household, and women should do as they are told. Men don't ask, they tell their wives what to do. The women just have to obey, or else they may be shouted at or sometimes even smacked. In extreme cases they may be sent back to their own family in disgrace, effectively being divorced. Nowadays, things have changed somewhat, thanks mainly to schooling, which is compulsory up to the end of primary school. Those women who have completed secondary school - or higher – are less likely to accept being treated this way but will speak back to their husbands without fear. From my observations, if a wife brings a wage into the family, her husband does not speak to her in the same way. Nevertheless, even well-educated women may be expected "to know their place", they can never be "above" their husbands.

A woman with education may also be able to find a job or set herself up in business, and gain financial independence. A woman of independent means can even leave her husband and live independently on her own income. Or, if she wishes, can return to her home village and live there the way she wants. This is what my younger sister, Maridhia, did when she had had enough of her husband's behaviour and attitude towards her and the children. Her husband was working in a Tanzanian city, so she returned to their home in her husband's village and started her own business. This thrived, so much so that she has built houses for herself and her children. When her husband retired, he found himself not very well off and he asked Maridhia to take him back. She wanted him to have the opportunity to be closer to his children as they grew up and so she agreed, but only on her terms. She made it clear she would not share a bedroom with him. She set strict rules for him; the tables were turned!

In contrast, I have a very close friend who didn't get much education, and her husband – who is well-educated - treats her like his maid. For example, she has never been allowed to know where in the house he keeps his money, even though they have been married for more than thirty years. When he does give her money he does so grudgingly, and it is never enough. She has been unable to live independently of her husband and she is stuck with him for the rest of her life, just because she didn't have the education that might have opened an opportunity to make her own money. She cannot even go back to her parents, because they are both dead. One of her daughters has the same problem with her husband. That is married life in Africa for you.

Traditionally, marriages were arranged between the families of the couple. They were not registered, and divorce was a relatively simple procedure. It might, however, involve the return of part of the dowry, which can make divorce more complicated depending on the length of time the couple have been together, and whether there are any children. In the case of my parents, the divorce was easy, because my father was Muslim. He simply had to repeat, 'I divorce you', three times in front of a witness, and that was that. In my mother and father's case, theirs was an amicable separation, and they kept in contact with each other and us, their children, throughout their lives, even though they both remarried. My father even attended my mother's funeral.

A divorced man with money or a steady job can easily attract a younger woman, and may be tempted to leave his wife. I know personally of two cases where this happened, and in both of them, the man later went back to his wife. The wives accepted the husband back, because they had no income, and therefore no option but to take what the man offered. On the other hand, a woman who is divorced will find it harder to attract a younger man. If she has no income of her own she may find herself having to marry an older man or becoming a second wife.

Women can become trapped in an abusive marriage when they have young children. It is hard for a woman to leave her children with a husband who cannot be trusted to take care of them. In many African cultures, including mine, women wishing to leave their husband are not permitted to take their children with them. An exception is only made when the husband has not paid the dowry in full, in which case she can take the children. Paying dowry gives the husband the right to keep the children. My parents provide an example. When they got divorced, because my father had paid all the dowry, my mother had no right to take us with her, though she was allowed to visit us, which she did regularly. When we were older, the restrictions were no longer enforced, and we stayed with her as long as we wanted. (Of course, when John and I got married, he paid all the dowry beforehand — joke!)

In Pare traditional culture, there are no laws restricting how many wives a man can have. The only limitation is that a man wishing to marry more than one wife must be able to pay the dowry for each one, and he must demonstrate that he is able to fully support them. Islam states that a man can marry up to four wives but only so long as he can afford to take care of them all. My grandfather — my mother's father — married eighteen wives, my grandmother being the sixth. He was a Muslim but clearly preferred to follow the traditional Pare rules over the Islamic ones! In his case, however, he was a tribal chief and possessed a considerable amount of land, which is the traditional measure of personal wealth.

You find more educated women in Kenya than in Tanzania, so Kenyan women are more likely to stand up for themselves than their Tanzanian sisters. They won't allow themselves to be worked like donkeys. This is not the case with all Kenyan women, however, there are still some unfortunate women whose husbands expect them to do all the menial tasks without a "please" or a "thank you". In the rare situations where a woman has to give her husband an instruction, she has to word it in such a way that it doesn't look as if she is telling him what to do. Above all, she must be polite. Some men, it seems, have very fragile egos.

This is a story of a woman in one of the villages I lived in as a teenager, who had discovered that her husband was cheating on her with other women. "Aren't I enough for you?" she asked him, to which he replied that he was very happy with her. 'Why, then, are you cheating on me with other women?' "Ah, well," he said, "I can't eat rice and beans every day, I like a bit of variety." "Well," she said, " I like variety too, so can I do the same?" The husband's answer was, "No, you can't, because you never paid dowry for me." Clearly, the man considered paying dowry as having "bought" his wife. Needless to say, this woman eventually left her husband.

In my opinion, the fact of having paid a dowry doesn't make a woman her husband's property. No one should put a price on any human being. It is just hard for those women who are left with no choice, and no voice.

Some women in the villages where I lived knew that their husbands were cheating on them, but accepted this behaviour. "Men will be men," they would say. Many believed leaving their husband and going back to their parents to be a worse alternative. A woman who does so has to face all sorts of difficulties. She may be looked down upon, unless she finds herself another man to marry, in most cases this would mean becoming a second or third wife. She may be accused of being a failure, even though it was the husband who behaved badly. For his part, he will merely marry a new, perhaps younger, wife. The woman who leaves her husband often cannot support herself, since by marrying, she may have lost any right that she might have had to her parents' land. If her husband had paid the dowry in full, she will also be deprived of the comfort and emotional support of her children, since they will have stayed with the husband unless they are younger than three. A married woman who cheats on her spouse will almost certainly be divorced. One rule for men and another for women.

MEN'S DUTY

Before I get accused of being "anti-men" (which I am not, by the way), I should point out that there are men who do work hard to support their families, but still within certain limits. For example, a man will never offer to cook a meal, or sweep the house, or clean up the cow dung, unless his wife is ill, or the man is unmarried. I know at least two men who say they intend to get married simply because they cannot cook — and they're not joking! The men are not to blame for this, since they have been raised this way. Even if, when young, they had wanted to go into the kitchen, it would have been strictly off limits. John and I have always encouraged our children to help with the cooking, and the most enthusiastic cook of the four of them was one of the sons.

If a wife is ill, her husband would ask one of their women neighbours to help. The neighbour would be happy to do so because it is the custom for people in the rural villages to support each other in all sorts of ways. Women will even fetch water for a neighbour who is unable to do so. It is not culturally acceptable for a man to carry anything on his head. Men either use a bicycle, or they carry the load on their shoulders. They don't even carry babies on their backs, only on their shoulders. When we went hiking in England, I was quite taken aback to meet men carrying babies, although even there, they tend to carry them on their front, in baby-carriers. This is a much better way of carrying a child, whether you are a woman or a man.

FORMS OF ADDRESS

In Kenya, married women and men do not call their spouses by their first names. Once, when I was on a visit to Kenya, I heard a woman make a slip of the tongue, and quite by accident call her husband by his first name. "Have you no respect for me?" he responded furiously. You are expected to address your husband or wife by the name of your child, preceded by "Mama" or "Baba." For example, if your child is called Rebecca, you would call your wife, "Mama Rebecca." The husband would be "Baba Rebecca." If you don't yet have children, you might say "Mpenzi wangu," meaning "my love."

Addressing someone older than you can be quite complicated. Even people who are only slightly older than you — four or five years or so — should be addressed as, "Kaka" (for men), or "Dada" (for women), meaning "Big brother" and "Big sister." The terms may be used for people who are not family members too, denoting affection or closeness. People who are more than fifty years old — whether family members or not — should be addressed as "Babuu," or "grandfather," while elderly women will be addressed as "Nyanya," or "Bibi," both meaning "grandma." When I first came to England I was horrified to hear married couples calling each other by their first names, just like children. Had they no respect for each other? Over time, I have learned not to judge other ways of behaving too hastily.

African houses

I spent my early years living in various thatched houses. These were simple dwellings with mud walls and thatched roofs. Some houses had corrugated iron roofs, which were more expensive and very hot. Thatched roofs are much cooler. As a child, however, I looked down on our house, believing it indicated how poor we were. Corrugated iron sheets looked smarter, and let more light in. A description of how these thatched houses were built can be found in my first book, *"A Tale for My Children and Grandchildren."* The main problem with thatched houses is that, although they are cooler, they provide a home for rats and snakes. Snakes and rats avoid corrugated iron roofs because they get too hot. Thatched houses generally have a ceiling, or part of one, on top of which people store their maize after harvesting. This maize attracts rats that eat it. Snakes then get in, on the hunt for the rats. Fine, you might say, rats killed, problem solved. The trouble is, snakes in Africa can be deadly, and it's not very comfortable living with a snake that might be venomous just above your head. It can be difficult to distinguish venomous and harmless snakes, so we tend to kill them if we see them.

If the house is situated in an open area, away from trees and long grass, there is less chance of snakes and rats getting in, not to mention the other creatures, such as millipedes, scorpions, centipedes, mosquitoes and safari ants. Sometimes it's nice to have a tree next to your home for the shade it gives. At the same time, trees are often home to some of the deadliest snakes, such as mambas. Life sometimes feels like one long battle against nature!

When we had been living in England for several years, my daughter Tuni and I went to Kenya and Tanzania to visit our extended family. We first went to Kenya, and stayed with Mr Bakari and his family in the village of Eldoro where I grew up. When we had been there for about three days Tuni, then thirteen, was keeping an eye on two young babies, twins, who were Mr Bakari's grandchildren. She suddenly noticed there was a snake in the roof, just above where the twins were lying on a mat on the floor. The snake was green, but a green snake can be either venomous or non-venomous. Tuni was terrified. She wanted to run out of the house, but she couldn't decide which baby to pick up. She couldn't carry both. She hesitated for a moment or two, then picked up one and ran outside. She began shouting for help. Fortunately she knew enough *Kiswahili* to tell people what had happened, and someone dashed into the house to pick up the other baby. I'm not sure what happened to the snake after that. I think it just disappeared back into the roof.

The houses in the village I lived in when I was a child are no longer thatched. They all have iron roofs, and some have been completely rebuilt with brick and plaster walls. These last longer than the mud-built houses. They look "smarter," more modern, are lighter inside and more airy, although the iron roofs make them hotter. Another disadvantage of an iron roof is that the sound of rain falling on it is incredibly loud. A heavy rainfall can be quite deafening, and you have to shout to make yourself heard.

MAASAI PEOPLE

One tribe that may be familiar to many people living outside Africa - from films or holiday visits to East Africa perhaps – is the Maasai. Even though there were Maasai near where I lived, I rarely interacted with them. They were often there in the background of my life but our paths rarely crossed. Unlike the *Wapare* they weren't settled in villages, but were nomadic, always on the move in search of pasture for their herds of cattle. Our two peoples didn't live entirely separate lives, however, and my first cousin was married to a Maasai man. Normally, when a Pare woman gets married, she is expected to leave her family and join that of her husband. In this case, however, the man left his family and joined my cousin's family. This is unusual but I have another more distant cousin who also married a Maasai man, and he too left his family to join the wife's. I think my cousins would have found it hard to live among the Maasai as their culture and way of life are very different from ours. There are many different tribes living in the area where I grew up but most of these actually have quite similar cultures, and marriages between them are not a great problem. Come to think of it, John and I come from very different cultures, but somehow we have managed — pretty well too! My first cousin's Maasai husband has become integrated into the *Wapare* way of life. He has learned to eat the food we eat, wear the same clothes, and is fluent in *Kipare*. I address him as *shemeji* (brother in-law). They have three children, who speak *Kipare* as their first language.

In recent years, the Maasai have become widely known thanks to TV. The young men, in their distinctive red clothes, dance holding their spears, jumping up and down and singing in the Maasai language. The women wear colourful, heavy bead necklaces, which bounce up and down as they dance. This particular style of dancing is peculiar to the Maasai, and is very different from that of the other tribes.

They are very good-looking, with smooth, shiny complexions and high cheekbones. Maasai men tend to be tall, slim and athletic. As a child, I was scared of them because the Maasai men always carried sticks whenever they were out walking. I was afraid they might beat me, like the schoolteachers did!

Their style of dress is very distinctive as compared with the other tribes. They wear a *kikoi*, which is striped — usually red and white — with fringes at each end, which is worn around the waist and over the shoulder. When I was a child, Maasai men wore the *kikoi* instead of trousers. The women wore layers consisting of different *kikois* in various colours and patterns with a red "cloak" over their shoulders that reached almost to the ground. Particularly distinctive are the very big, heavy earrings. These don't just hang from the lobes but from almost any part of the ear and are made of beads or other colourful stones. Women often have wooden earplugs which, over time, stretch the earlobe to form a large loop, hanging almost to their shoulders. Not just ears are treated this way. I have seen a Maasai lady whose lower lip had been stretched until the loop hung down below her chin. Notions of beauty are different in different cultures, and there is no "proper" standard of what is or is not considered beautiful.

Nowadays some Maasai do cultivate plots of land, but mostly they still herd cows. The spears they hold when they are dancing are not just decorative but are also carried when they are out herding their cows. They are weapons used to defend the cattle from lions. Because they are constantly on the move, Maasai houses are made of mud and thatch that are not so different from those of the *Wapare* in the villages in my youth, but are much simpler and easier to put up and take down.

The Maasai diet consists of raw meat, milk straight from the cow, and on special occasions, blood obtained by spearing the neck of a cow, draining some blood and then plastering the wound with mud to stop the bleeding. A person's wealth is judged by the number of cattle he has. Members of my family who live in a small village called Mata, on the margin of the Tsavo National Park, told me that the Maasai are reputed to be cattle rustlers. According to the Maasai, cattle were created for them; all cattle belong to them and they are simply reclaiming what is rightfully theirs! It is a common excuse for starting a war, even today.

I have never personally witnessed a Maasai marriage ceremony. Some former schoolmates of mine sent me a video from Kenya, about two Maasai men who both fell in love with the same girl. The girl in question did not mind which one she married because she found both equally attractive. The two men decided to fight each other for her hand in marriage. The victor was able to marry the girl and pass on his "strong" genes.

I went to school with people from many different tribes but never a Maasai. Nowadays almost all Maasai boys attend school, though not the girls. People from many tribes, including mine, consider that sending girls to school is a waste of resources. They reason that girls will get married and leave their homes, bringing no benefit to their family, whereas boys remain in the family home and support their parents in their old age. Sadly, this attitude is still prevalent today. In 2021, over a quarter of all secondary schoolgirls in Tanzania had to leave school because they fell pregnant. Pregnancy is common even amongst primary schoolgirls. This in turn causes parents to be even more reluctant to send their daughters to school. Mostly, the men (or boys) involved deny all responsibility for the pregnancy. We women still face a big struggle to make life fair for us all.

Kenyan tribes

As a Kenyan, I have always been aware of my country's ethnic diversity; it was an everyday part of my life. Even in our small village of Eldoro contained people from at least five different tribes. When I began to travel further afield I met people from many different ethnic groups, not just African tribes, such as the *Mijikenda* and the *Wadigo* near the coast, but Indians, Arabs and Europeans too. There are, in fact, over forty tribes in Kenya. The largest tribes, such as the *Kikuyu, Luo, Luhya* and *Kamba,* number in the millions. My own tribe, the *Wapare,* is relatively small in comparison.

In Eldoro village where I lived with my aunt Khadija, the tribes in the area had a lot in common. We were all farmers, growing similar crops — maize, kidney beans, yams, cassava, sugar cane, cabbages, spinach and all the local fruits. Although we grew similar crops, different ethnic groups cooked them in slightly different ways. There is a saying in *Kiswahili, "Wali mmoja, mapishi mbalimbali."* The literal meaning is "One rice, different ways of cooking." We learned the various ways of cooking from each other, not by exchanging recipes, but by watching people while they prepared them. For example, pilau is a dish made from rice mixed with chicken or beef and lots of different spices. In Kenya, it probably originated among the *Waswahili,* who live on the coast, and we have learned from them how to prepare it. But the *Waswahili* themselves adopted it from the Arabs who traded along the East African Coast. I am told that in Spain there is a similar dish called pilaf. I will leave you to think about how that got there!

Although the people of each tribe spoke their own mother tongue, we were still able to communicate with each other using *Kiswahili,* the national language of both Kenya and Tanzania. My mother tongue is *Kipare.* Marriage between people from different ethnic backgrounds has become more common in today's Kenya, perhaps because people travel more and live in urban areas with a mixed population. To my surprise I have discovered that most of the younger members of my family have not married a Pare but someone from a different tribe. A quick count turned up marriage partners from amongst the *Wataita, Wamasai, Wadigo, Waswahili, Wakamba, Wachagga, Wazungu,* and probably there are others too.

A major factor dividing the people living in Eldoro is religion, since we have both Muslims and Christians in the village. The Muslims go to their mosques to pray and the Christians go to their various churches, but we still invite each other to celebrations, such as weddings, at the end of the fast of Ramadan, or when the Christians are celebrating Christmas. If you are open-minded enough, a chance to feast and celebrate is not to be turned down! The only issue that I have experienced is that strict Muslims will need to know whether the meat that is served is Halal, that is, killed in the right way. But even if the meat is not Halal, they will still join in, eating the other foods on offer.

Greetings

Wapare greet each other by shaking hands - but never using the left hand. Pare culture does not encourage a male and a female adult to hug each other although it is quite common for two men or two women to hug each other. It is almost taboo for a man to have bodily contact - beyond hand-shaking - with a woman who is not his wife. Even contact by an adult man with his own mother or an older sister is very much discouraged. Boys under the age of about ten can hug their mothers. Hugging your own son when he gets older seems to be forbidden, which I think is a shame. However, I am allowed to hug my brother-in-law, and John is allowed to hug my sister; we can even joke with each other. I think this may be to do with what is allowed in Pare culture if a husband or wife dies, especially when there are young children in their family. If a man dies leaving a wife and children, his brother is allowed to marry the widowed wife, although generally as a second or subsidiary wife. This is what happened when my half-brother passed away leaving a wife and family; his younger brother married his former sister-in-law, and later he also married the wife of his choice. The two wives do not, however, live in the same household. If a wife dies leaving young children, the widower can marry whoever he chooses as a stepmother for those children.

We have rather wandered away from the subject of greetings, but that is likely to happen as I write my life's patchwork quilt.

Now that I no longer live in Africa, I am happy that I can hug my sons and grandsons, and also my sons-in-law.

My African family would disapprove, but hugging is my way of showing them that I love and care about them. I'm sure some African people reading this may be thinking I have been influenced by Western culture. Possibly they are right. I'm sure that if I had remained in Kenya, especially in my village, I would have behaved according to African cultural expectations. Now, when I go to Tanzania, I do hug my uncle, which I would not have done in the past, and I sometimes hold his hand when we are walking together. It is interesting that he doesn't object to this. If I have changed through living abroad, why has he changed? It could be that Pare culture has been changing in my absence but I notice that my uncle only relaxes the rules with me, not with his own daughters. My guess is that he thinks that my being married to a '*mzungu*' (a white man) makes me a bit of a *mzungu* too, so he accepts my unusual behaviour.

I am a little bit sad that I only once hugged my father, and that was on his deathbed. That hug is a memory that I will always treasure.

Traditional Marriage in Kenya and Tanzania

In the 1970s, when my schooldays were almost over, I discovered that a senior member of the family was trying to arrange a marriage for me to a man who lived in Moshi and was already married with a family., He had decided he wanted a second wife. Because he had the same religious beliefs, my family member told him I might make a suitable second wife. I was not aware of this at the time and I only heard about it later, from the man himself. By the time they were ready to begin the negotiations, I had given birth to a child. This put him off and he lost interest. I had a lucky escape, although I would have refused to marry him anyway, if I had known what was being discussed. There was no way I was going to be a second wife, especially to a man I hardly knew. Furthermore, I simply was not attracted to him, so he was disqualified on two counts!

In the past, it was common practice for marriages to be arranged in this way. Usually, the parents of a boy would start looking for a wife for their son. They would consider not just the character of the girl, but also her family background. Did the family get on well with their neighbours? Did any members of the family have a reputation for some sort of bad behaviour? And so on. Once they had identified a girl that they approved of, they would sit down with their son and ask him what he thought of this girl, and whether or not he liked her. If the boy said he was interested, he was encouraged to talk to her and get to know her better and to see if there was mutual attraction.

The boy would then tell his parents how he felt about her, and whether he would like her as a wife. If he was not interested in her, his parents might still try to persuade him to marry her. If this failed, and the boy still refused, the matter would end there. If he was agreeable, the boy's parents would arrange to visit the parents of the girl. The boy and girl themselves were not involved. A family member would be sent to pass on the message — in my aunt's time and when I was young, no one had a telephone, never mind a mobile phone. Indeed there were people who did not know how to read and write. The message would read something like this: "We are... and we would like to visit you on…" The girl's family would be aware of the purpose of this visit, and the two sets of parents would begin the discussions.

Girls weren't supposed to look for a future husband, only boys looked for a wife. Now that so many women are educated, this has changed. For one thing, boys and girls attend school together, often meeting other children from different backgrounds. This was my experience, and I found it quite liberating. For those children who go to boarding school, which is quite common in Kenyan rural areas in particular, the weakening of family influence and the impact of meeting girls and boys of a similar age is even greater.

Once the boy's parents had been given a date by the girl's parents, they would prepare themselves by choosing some gifts to take. In African tradition, you do not visit friends or family empty-handed. When you are visiting your prospective in-laws, the presents will be selected with even greater care. The parents of the boy have to make sure they are well-dressed so as to impress the girl's family. They greet one another with a big smile and a handshake — not a hug. The boy's parents are invited into the sitting room, invited to take seats and offered a drink, probably *chai* (tea), perhaps served with *mandazi* (home-made doughnuts). If the boy's parents are expected for lunch, they will be served rice and stewed chicken or beef, or *sima* with stewed chicken or even the traditional Pare dish, *Kishumba,* which is made from green bananas with red kidney beans. The bananas are peeled, chopped and boiled in a *sufuria* (pan). When the bananas are cooked, the red kidney beans are mixed in with them. It is very tasty if cooked in the right way, but too much *Kishumba* can give you wind! *Kishumba* is usually only provided when you can't afford meat, chicken or fish.

Once the visitors have finished the food they have been eating, they will hand over the gifts they have brought. They might include a pair of *lessos,* which are brightly coloured lengths of cloth, which women wear wrapped around the waist, like a sarong. Only then will the boy's parents initiate the conversation regarding a possible marriage between the two young people. It is usually the father of the boy who begins, saying something like, "My wife and I are here to visit you both, because we have a he goat and the he goat is looking for a she goat." Although the girl's parents are perfectly aware of the reason for the visit, a long silence will then ensue, while the girl's parents think about the proposal. Eventually, they will respond with, "We hear you but we won't give you an answer until we have spoken to our daughter." They would then ask a few questions, such as the name of the boy, and what he does for a living. The boy's parents will then go away and wait for the answer. Several days later, the girl's parents will send a messenger to invite the boy's parents to come and hear their decision.

The boy's parents will try to judge whether the answer to their proposal will be a "Yes" or a "No" from their reception by the girl's parents. A big smile and a friendly handshake are often enough to show that the answer is positive, though not always, of course. Suppose they are mistaken, they may wonder, "What if the girl's parents are just being polite?" Still anxious, they are shown into the sitting room and offered *chai* or a soft drink. When everyone is seated, drinks in their hands, the girl's parents will give their response. If it is positive, further discussion ensues. The first item often concerns the two families' religion. Naturally, both will prefer the couple to share the same religion. The parents of the girl will also ask more about the boy's financial situation — can he afford to provide for her?

The girl's parents will also want to find out about the boy's extended family. Are they "good," that is law-abiding people? Are they perhaps corrupt? If the family is well-off, how did they get to that position? Some people can get rich through corruption or thieving, so it is important for the girl's parents to ask these questions, even though they might want other confirmation of any claims to innocence. Many other things will be taken into account. How much land do they own? Land ownership has always been important to Africans, for any number of reasons. Not only is land a source of food and income, it also reflects a person's status. When John proposed marriage to me, my family were shocked to hear that he didn't own a single piece of land, not even a house. How would we live?

Once the two sets of parents have come to an agreement, the boy and the girl will be allowed to meet, and find out how they feel about each other. If they are both happy, all well and good. If not, they might be given more time to think about it. If they still don't get along, the matter is brought to a close. The boy's parents will have to look for another girl and go through the whole procedure again. By the time it has reached this stage, however, it usually ends well, at least partly because the parents are very unlikely to have embarked on negotiations if they thought there was little chance of success.

If the boy and the girl practise different religions, a compromise will have to be reached. In such cases it is usually the girl who is expected to adopt her future husband's religion. Girls from a strict Muslim family usually can only marry another Muslim. If the boy is not a Muslim negotiations may still continue if the couple are deeply in love and there is a possibility of one of them changing religion. Otherwise, conversations about the marriage will cease. Muslim parents, at least those from Kenya and Tanzania, are not so strict these days. My own marriage is a case in point. John is not a Muslim, yet my father was happy to agree to the marriage. He strongly believed that his children should be allowed to marry whoever they chose. My mother, Mwanaima, and my aunt, Khadija, agreed with him, and were always very supportive. I shall always be grateful to them for that.

Once it is certain that the marriage will go ahead, preparations for the wedding begin. A few days beforehand, the girl will have her hair carefully plaited in the style of her choice, perhaps a heart shape. Her hands will be decorated with henna, which symbolises good health and prosperity in marriage. In some cultures, such as my own, the darker the henna stain, the deeper the love it symbolises. As in many cultures, the bride will have a wedding dress made. Although, these days, European-style, long white wedding dresses may be worn by urban, Christian brides in particular, these are not traditional to East African. In the villages at least, when I was younger, the bride's dress was long, reaching her ankles, but brightly coloured. The bridegroom will wear a suit that can be worn again, unlike the bride's wedding dress. The groom's hair will be cut very short.

It is the man that marries, and not the woman. For example, I am married by John, but John is not married by me – he marries me. The man plays an active role in the marriage and the woman is passive. On the surface, this might seem just a matter of semantics, but I think it is another example the way African men see women; through the act of marriage, a man's wife "belongs" to him, marriage is something done to her. Similarly, a woman whose religion is different to that of her prospective husband is expected to give up her faith, but he never does.

Arranged marriages are much less common today. Girls can now choose a husband for themselves, as I did. Many people frowned upon my marriage to John because I was marrying a European and a non-believer. Well, I have proved them all wrong — marrying John was the best decision I have ever made.

When I was younger, a girl could not openly express her feelings for a boy. She would have to make her feelings known through her body language — a smile, eye contact, and even a wink if she was brave enough. Nowadays, many young people have mobile phones, communicating by text or WhatsApp without their parents knowing what they are saying or who they are saying it to. Acquaintances and friendships made at school can be continued out of school without parents' knowledge, sometimes leading eventually to identifying a marriage partner. This is less likely to be the case for girls from rural areas, especially those with little education.

At the time when I was a teenager, girls were not supposed to sleep with any man before marriage. Still today, most African men want to marry a virgin, which is why some men prefer to marry young girls. (In the past, in some tribes, girls – but not boys – would be married off at sixteen - or even younger. Nowadays, both Kenya and Tanzania have a legal minimum age for marriage set at 17 or 18 years.) The same taboo on sex before marriage still does not apply to men, who can sleep with as many women as they want. Often, "sleeping around" is considered something to be proud of, and shows how virile a man is. It is those men who want power and control over women.

Nowadays, many parents, especially the well-educated, prefer to leave their sons or daughters to make their own choice of marriage partner. The two sets of parents will then not be involved until much later, when the boy or the girl have already decided. Boys, however, are more likely than girls to "shop around," as the saying goes. Having no experience of this in my own life, I have had to rely on friends to tell me what this involves. The boy probably starts his choice with the more attractive girls and only then looks for personality and good nature. Lastly, he considers the girl's family and its status. He may meet with six or more girls, I am told, before deciding which one he likes best. The two then meet by themselves, away from other people. The boy initiates the conversation, expressing his feelings for the girl. The girl might be expected to act shy — perhaps she really is — but by agreeing to meet like this she has shown that she is perfectly well aware of the boy's intentions. Her eyes on the ground, never once meeting the boy's gaze, she may respond that she likes him, too. Her parents will have told her not to fully trust a boy's initial expression of love — he may be more interested in sex than marriage. If she thinks he is genuinely interested in marriage, she will agree to meet him again. Some girls are brought up never to say "yes" to a boy's first proposal. In *Wapare* tradition, the boy must ask a girl at least four times before she takes him seriously. The couple will continue to see each other many times before their parents are informed.

The boy's parents will then arrange to meet the girl's parents to inform them that their son would like to marry their daughter. A process of negotiation similar to that for an arranged marriage then takes place. In normal circumstances, this should proceed smoothly. If the girl's parents dislike the boy for any reason, there is not much they can do about it, since it is not an arranged marriage, though they may present difficulties, causing the process to take longer. They may be reluctant to support their daughter's choice of husband because he doesn't have a well-paid job. In the end, it's up to the girl and the boy to make the final decision. A girl from my extended family found herself in this position. She went ahead and married the boy and has lived perfectly happily with him, giving birth to three children.

In almost all African societies, a man has to pay a dowry to the girl's parents before the marriage can go ahead. The amount to be paid will depend on the girl's level of education: the more educated she is, the higher the amount, although it is always subject to negotiation. The dowry does not always have to be paid in full before the marriage, but this varies from one family to another. The dowry will not only consist of cash. For example, when John and I got married, my parents demanded a dowry of a cow, some goats, some cash, a blanket for my grandmother and a lorry-load of firewood. Because John did not own any beasts, he was allowed to pay the price of the cow and goats in cash, but this was unusual. Needless to say, John definitely wasn't "buying" me! And not long after we married, my father gave our children some of his own cows. In our case, the dowry was more symbolic, an indication of the bond between our two families.

LIVING TOGETHER

In East Africa, it was practically taboo for a boy and a girl to live together without being married and it is still disapproved of. When I was working in Britain, I was shocked to hear a British colleague saying, "Oh yes, my daughter is living with her boyfriend."In the culture I was brought up in, no parent would ever openly admit to such a thing, it was considered embarrassing, even shameful. If a young man and woman did start living together before they were married, it was assumed it would eventually — preferably as soon as possible – lead to marriage. Both sets of parents would put pressure on the couple to get married.

As always seems to be the case, it will be the woman who suffers most from such an arrangement if the relationship doesn't work out, especially if she gets pregnant. It will be is harder for the young woman to find another young man to marry, as she is seen as "damaged goods." As far as the young man is concerned, previous sexual experience does not affect his future prospects — the old double standard! As for the woman, she will have no option but to return to her family with the baby, bringing them an extra mouth to feed. However, it is important to point out that the baby will still be welcomed and loved; it is the mother and her future prospects that suffer, not the child. The child only suffers if his or her father refuses to contribute to the school fees and other educational expenses. Even then, the mother's family may step in where they are able.

Some men, however, have no other choice but to marry a woman who has slept with another man, or who is divorced. Traditionally, it is the man who actively seeks out a future wife, and never the woman. A girl who approaches a man is considered much too "forward." An educated man probably won't even look at woman who has had no education, leaving her with little choice as to whom to marry. I know of a young man from my village who struggled at primary school and left barely knowing how to read or write. He didn't have many friends. His parents arranged a marriage for him with a woman who had even less education. They now live happily together, on a small piece of land where they grow their own food. Education isn't everything!

My views on living together before marriage have changed over the years. I have come to believe that living together gives the two people involved a better chance to get to know each other before committing themselves for life. In Kenyan and Tanzanian society, people are more likely to get to know each other through the intermediary of friends or family members, rather than direct personal acquaintance. In my opinion this is not a reliable approach to such an important decision. Of course, it is also important that a third person does not also come into consideration here, namely a baby. In the past, in Kenya, contraception was not easily available for unmarried women so that living together before marriage involved the risk of getting pregnant. Living together as an effective way of finding out about each other depends in part on the easy availability of contraception!

Sometimes the couple decides to elope. The girl quietly disappears from her home and goes to live with the boy at his parents' home. If this situation arises, then it is the responsibility of the boy's parents to tell those of the girl where their daughter has gone. Once a girl has run away and slept with her boyfriend, the damage is done. The four parents sit down together, sort out their differences, accept the situation and allow the girl and the boy to live together and, hopefully, get married after the dowry has been agreed upon.

MARRIAGE AND CHILDREN

In the 1960s, when I lived in Kitoghoto and later in Eldoro, married women gave birth to as many children as they could; 'the more the better' was their view. Children were seen as a blessing from God. This may seem irresponsible when existence is such a struggle. Why do you want to have more mouths to feed? The answer is complicated.

First of all, poor people are more likely to suffer from serious illnesses — especially malaria — and health care services are generally either poor or expensive. People could never be sure how many of their children will survive to adulthood. Furthermore, in countries with no state pension or other form of government support, parents rely on their grown-up children to support them in their old age. So, the more you have, the more secure you feel about your future. Infant mortality rates were high in those days but are much lower now. It is interesting, therefore, that as health services have improved, many more children survive and the number of children born to each woman has decreased a lot.

Then there is the question of contraception, which in rural villages, just isn't available. Even when I was a teenager, or even older, no one ever talked about contraception. Schools generally did not provide much sex education and the topic contraception may not have been covered at all. (Since the appearance of HIV / AIDS, the use of condoms became a major topic, but as a prophylaxis, not as a contraceptive.) I remember being taught about "safe times" to avoid pregnancy, but contraception was never mentioned. Parents certainly never discussed such matters with their daughters. We were simply told not to do it! When contraception did become available in the villages, it was never offered to unmarried women. A married woman could get contraception, but only if she was accompanied by her husband, who had to give his permission for his wife to use contraception. I had a friend whom I will call "Rehema" who lived in my village. Having had four or five children, she did not want any more, so she asked the husband to go with her to the doctor, but he refused. Rehema had no alternative but to refuse to sleep with him. The husband said, "Fine, I'll find another wife," which he did. I am not sure if he had children with his second wife.

In my experience, most religions preached against the use of contraception, or at least discouraged it. It is not surprising, therefore, that families tended to be large, and large numbers of girls and young women fell pregnant. These days, the situation has improved, and there is less social resistance to the use of contraception. Women who do choose to limit the number of children they have tend – once again - to be more educated. I remember asking a family friend — an educated woman — if she was going to have more children than the two she already had. Her answer was a very definite, "No!" She was fortunate in that she could make that decision for herself without asking her husband's permission.

CHILDREN OUTSIDE OF MARRIAGE

Sometimes when a boy makes an unmarried girl pregnant and refuses to take any responsibility for the child, the mother will be left to raise it alone. If she has no income, this can be a nightmare. Finding another man when you have already have a child by someone else, might prove to be difficult. I have known some men who marry a woman who already has a child (or children) from a previous relationship. They adopted the children because they were truly in love with the woman. This is not a formal adoption but an acceptance of the child as part of the family. On the other hand, some men are reluctant to raise another person's child and will not accept taking care of an extra one. This may be because they think they will find it difficult to bond with the child, especially if they go on to have their own children with the woman.

Men are often more willing to accept a female child than a male. This is because a girl is seen as a "temporary" member of her birth family, since she will marry and join her future husband's family. Also, when male children reach adulthood, they will expect a share of the family land. Traditionally, land is owned and passed on through the male line, so the presence of an "outside" male child can mean loss of "family land." In this situation, it is up to the mother to make the decision whether to marry the man — leaving her child with her parents — or to keep the child. If the mother's parents are able to take care of the child, then the child will remain with them or possibly with other relatives.

My second cousin had a boy child before she was married. She left her son with her parents because her husband-to-be did not want to adopt the child. He claimed that he did not want to look after a child who is not of his own blood. Although my second cousin left her son with her parents, she makes sure she sees him regularly and takes him food and clothing, while also supporting her parents. The child will be supported fully and when he is ready to go to school, his uncle will help with paying his school fees — if he can afford it.

My mother's second husband already had one wife. My younger sister, Maridhia, was at the time living with another aunt in Tanzania and was crying for our mother because she was too young to stay without either of her parents. So my mother took Maridhia to live with her and her second husband, who made it clear to my mum that, "Yes, Maridhia can live with us, but I will not be responsible for her clothes or her school fees, although I am happy to provide food for her." My dad, being conscious of his responsibilities, did not expect another man to bring up his daughter. He was happy that Maridhia was able to live with our mother for some years, at least until she finished her schooling.

When Maridhia went to live with our mother and her stepfather, I went to live in Kenya with my father's half-sister, my aunt Khadija, who had no children of her own. My mother could not take both of us with her to her new family and, since I was the elder sister, she felt I could adjust more easily to living with my aunt. My Aunt Khadija became a much-loved second mother to me. Being the only child, I was the main focus of her attention and probably got spoiled!

Aunt Khadija

When I was growing up, I asked my aunt Khadija, what getting married was like when she was young. Back then, she said, most marriages were arranged. Young girls were expected to remain a virgin until they got married. The family of the bride would be informed shortly after the wedding ceremony whether their daughter had proved to be a virgin or not. The people attending the ceremony — including both sets of parents — would be invited by the "best man" as he is known in England, but not in East Africa — to have a soft drink (alcohol was not usually served). After a while, it would be announced that the bride and groom were going to "have a little rest" in one of the rooms, which had been prepared with white bed-linen. The newly married couple would spend about an hour together in bed, making love, while the guests waited to be shown proof of the bride's virginity. If it was indeed the bride's first time to make love, it was expected to be uncomfortable or even painful. The "best man" listened outside the door to hear her scream, and when it was over, he took the white sheet, with blood on it, outside and showed it to the assembled guests, especially both sets of parents. If there was no blood, it would bring shame upon the whole of the bride's family. If the evidence showed that she was indeed a virgin, drums would be beaten, and the wedding guests would begin to celebrate. The women in the bride's family would dance and ululate.

Couples sometimes cheat, according to my aunt. If the man has been responsible for her losing her virginity before they got married, the couple will collect some blood — perhaps from a slaughtered chicken — and put it in a small bottle. They will smuggle the bottle into the "restroom" and smear the sheet with the blood.

According to Aunt Khadija, if there was no blood, meaning that the bride was not a virgin, it would bring shame upon the whole family. The girl's story would be talked about in the village for a long time to come, an embarrassment for the husband, who might choose at some point to marry another girl. Islam permits a man to have up to four wives, so long as he can afford to take care of them. Many men take more than one wife even if the first was a virgin. A woman, on the other hand, cannot have four husbands. I believe that in Tibet, at least up to the 1930s, a woman could marry up to four men, as long as they are all brothers. It must have been difficult to know which child belonged to which man!

Marriage changes the status of both partners. The woman is no longer a girl, and the boy becomes a man. The woman will now be referred to as the wife of Mr so-and-so. She will "belong" to her husband, who is still called by his name. When a woman has a child, she is known as "Mama (mother) so-and-so," while the husband is addressed as "Baba (father) of…" Very rarely are women or men referred to by their first names, except perhaps by someone of a similar age. If the married couple are childless, the woman is called "dada" (sister), the man being "uncle" or "brother." Recently, a cousin of mine accidentally called her husband by his first name; he responded angrily. "How dare you call me that! Have you no respect for me?"

This leads me to a bit of a side line about how to address individuals, but this is probably as good a place as any to cover it. Using the correct form of address can be complicated in many societies. When I had not been long in England, I was horrified when my eight-year-old nephew addressed me as "Aisha". Had he no respect for me? It took me quite a while to understand that this was not done out of disrespect, although I still get a bit startled when it happens. In East Africa, calling an older person by their first name is taboo. Only children are free to use one another's first names. An important part of growing up in East Africa is learning how to address different people, depending on their age or relationship. On meeting a stranger, I have to estimate their age in relation to mine; then I may call them "dada" (sister), "mama" (for an older woman), or "nyanya" or "bibi" if they are much older. The equivalents for men are "kaka", "baba" and "babuu."

Women are expected to become pregnant within the first year of their marriage. If this fails to occur, it is always assumed to be the woman who is at fault, hardly ever the man. In my aunt Khadija's time, and even when I was a young woman, no one would think of going to see a doctor if they have a problem conceiving. If, over time, the woman still does not conceive, the man will look for another wife. My aunt Khadija is an example. She had a daughter who died when she was very young, but did not conceive again, so her husband, Mzee Zuberi, married another woman. Unlike most men, Mzee Zuberi was considerate enough to ask her permission to marry another wife so that he might not die childless. For her part, my aunt accepted his reasoning, and agreed that he could take another wife. This was very unusual back then. Mzee Zuberi took a second wife who bore him three children, two boys and a girl. My aunt Khadija was very supportive of her, and made sure that she settled well in the family home.

If a woman finds herself unhappy during her first year of marriage, perhaps because her husband has been unfaithful, she has the right to leave him before they have too many children. Her family should support her decision. The problem with courtship in our African culture is that it does not allow a couple to get to know each other better before they are married. Both the man and the woman do their best to impress each other, and never get to understand what their prospective partner is really like. In cases where they find they are incompatible, the woman is always the loser. It will be harder for her to find another man to marry.

One of my cousins married a man she hardly knew. She only discovered what her husband was really like after several months. He drank, and ran after other women. My cousin left him and returned to her family home, even though she was already pregnant. To this day, her former husband has never been to see his son, and I am told he hasn't changed his ways. Their son is doing well and is being supported by my cousin's family. If they had had the opportunity to live together, or at least spend time alone together before getting married, I really believe that my cousin would not have married this man. In my opinion, our African culture presents a problem in not allowing a couple to live together before marriage.

But what if the woman becomes pregnant before marriage? Given the attitude towards and poor availability of contraception, this often happens. More often than not, a married woman who leaves her husband has no right to take the child with her; many African societies consider children as belonging to the husband, not the wife. In my cousin's case, however, she was able to keep her son because her husband hadn't paid the full dowry. If a woman leaves her husband and he has paid the full dowry, he can claim his dowry back, unless they have been married for more than two years. If he decides not to claim the dowry back, he can still claim his child, even after many years.

Another reason why some African men may marry

more than one wife is the need to have a son. In Eldoro, a *Chaga* lady married to a Kenyan man gave birth to three girls. Her husband wanted at least one son, and so he divorced her and married another woman. His second wife gave him two sons. Meanwhile, the divorced wife had married again and became a second wife. Ironically, she then had sons.

DIVORCE

In those parts of Africa that I am familiar with, divorce is a simple procedure, much more so than in the West. This is particularly true for Muslim couples, as I know from the example of my own parents. My mother and father got divorced when I was very young, so I had no idea what was involved, until my father told me when I was about eight. All he had to do was say "I divorce you" three times, in front of a witness.

Nowadays, divorce is not quite so simple because of changes in the marriage laws. Marriage these days is more than an agreement between two families; it is a legal agreement. There are documents to be signed and conditions to be met, so the whole thing takes longer.

Sometimes a man may regret his actions and wish to remarry his estranged wife. I know a man who divorced his wife and married another woman. After some years, he realised he had made a mistake, and asked his previous wife if she was willing to get back together. She was still in love with him, so they got married again, and he ended up with two wives. The second wife wasn't happy about it, but she had no choice in the matter. Now the two wives live in different compounds, and have separate households.

After divorcing my mother, my father married a younger woman with whom he went on to have six children — three boys and three girls. My mother also got married again, to a much older man than my father, and they had three children — a boy and two girls. Fortunately, I get on well with all of my half-sisters and half-brothers. We don't even call each other half-sister or half-brother, just sisters and brothers.

Wedding Rings

In my time, people did not exchange rings when they got married — most people couldn't afford one. That was the case with John and I. We only bought rings some time after we came to England. We arrived with four children, two suitcases containing all our possessions, and only three hundred pounds between us, so we had more important things to worry about! Even now, most of the couples in my African family do not have wedding rings. Nowadays, a few couples are getting married according to the rites they have learned about from the West, but it is not our culture. For one thing, it would be very expensive to buy rings for four wives, unless a man is very rich!

I will tell you a story of a man who occupied a very senior position in the Kenyan government. He married three wives, and gave each one a nice car, and a large piece of land with a big house on it. Servants took care of all the chores. His children went to private schools — chauffeur-driven, not on foot like the rest of us. The man shared his attentions equally among the three wives, who were all very content. Then disaster struck, and the man was suddenly taken ill and died. Each wife wanted him to be buried on her land. The respective families gathered together to try to resolve the problem.

After a long and heated discussion, someone suggested that the husband should be cut into three pieces, and each piece buried on each of the three wives' land. The first wife agreed to this solution. She suggested that, because she was the first wife, she should be the first to choose which piece of her husband would be hers. She declared that she would choose the head, because of her husband's romantic eyes and warm lips. The second wife said she would take the middle part, because of her husband's big heart (and perhaps his big wallet). The third wife said she was happy to take the bottom part, because it would remind her of the romantic times she had had with him in bed!

At this point, a senior government official intervened, declaring that he had never heard of such a barbaric way of settling a dispute. According to government regulations, he said, only the first wife could be accepted as the official wife. In the end, his decision was upheld, the first wife was the winner, and the husband was buried on her land, leaving the second and third wives disappointed. I guess in every situation someone has to win and others have to lose. That's life!

PREGNANCY AND CHILDBIRTH

In Africa women are generally expected to keep working throughout pregnancy, right up to the moment when they give birth. The work is hard, too, they are not spared from fetching water, carrying firewood, digging the ground. A woman who dares to complain may be told, "Pregnancy does not affect your hands, does it, so why not use them?" There are no expectations, as there seems to be in the West, that a pregnant woman should take things easy. On the other hand, once the baby is born, it is the custom among my people for mother and child to stay in the house for forty days. After that, the mother, accompanied by a family member, takes the baby to have its first haircut. Mother and baby then spend a further three months together, resting in the house. During this time, the women of the family cook special food for the mother — millet porridge, for example — so as to make sure she can produce enough milk for the baby. At the end of the three months, the mother may leave the house and start helping with the lighter chores, such as washing her and her baby's clothes. She may go to the river to fetch water, leaving the baby with another family member. The baby can now be taken outside, but must be kept in the shade, out of the sun. (You might think that Africans cannot get sunburned but, believe me, we can — especially a baby!)

Mothers usually breastfeed their babies until they are four or five months old, when they will be fed pureed food until they have finished teething. Nobody in the rural villages has a liquidiser. Instead, the baby's food is mashed with a little milk or warm water using a wooden spoon. Some mothers give their babies food they have first chewed — maize is often given this way since it can't be easily mashed with a spoon. When the babies have enough teeth, they will be given solid food, such as sweet potatoes, cooked bananas and *sima*, the staple, with vegetables, or perhaps meat or fish stew. Mothers breastfeed their babies until they begin to walk, sometimes longer than that. My aunt Khadija told me she was breastfed until she was almost five. By then her mother wasn't producing any milk, she used it as a comforter, something like the "comfort" blankets children in the West might have. She would order her mother, *Itekaa thi ambu nienda kuamwa* (sit down, I want to suckle).

It's the responsibility of the mother to decide what sort of food to give to her baby or toddler. If she is not around for some reason, another family member will choose and cook something appropriate. This person will usually be a woman, although in some cases it might be the father of the child.

Once a baby has begun to crawl, she or he has to be watched. Babies everywhere pick up whatever they find, and it goes straight into their mouth. In the rural villages this is likely to include animal droppings, from hens, goats, sheep and so on. Every morning early, the mother of the household sweeps the ground surrounding the house, but it is impossible to keep it completely clear. The presence of dung also means dung beetles, fascinating for a little child.

If there is no one available to keep an eye on the baby, the mother straps the infant onto her back with a *lesso*, and gets on with her tasks. Columns of safari ants are another danger, since in a twinkling of an eye these ants will cover any living thing in their path, and a young toddler could easily be killed if the ants are not seen and swept away quickly. Safari ants can suffocate small animals, such as kittens. I have known this happen but I have no experience of children being killed – attacked, yes, but not killed, as there will always be someone nearby to hear the baby's cries if an attack happens.

(John has reminded me of the day he got up early, still dozy, and wandered into the kitchen to put the kettle on. He felt something creeping over his bare feet, looked down and found he was standing in the middle of wide column of safari ants which were nibbling at him as they progressed up his legs. The only way to deal with them was to sweep them outside as quickly as possible – not an easy task in itself as they hold on to the broom. Once they are out of the house the only way to stop them returning is to spread charcoal ashes all around the outside of the house.)

Once the baby is moving around the house and outside, looking out for such dangers is just another task for the mother. (John can look after himself!)

Teething and herbal remedies

To ease a teething child's discomfort, mothers use herbs, which they rub on the baby's gums. If the herbs don't help, then the children will be taken to the local clinic. Herbal remedies are still used to treat all kinds of ailments, from a cough to a stomach-ache. Their effectiveness depends on how severe the pain is. My parents knew so many different medicinal plants and how to prepare them. Whenever my brother had a stomachache, my mother would gather the roots from a certain plant and boil them in water. The mixture was left to cool down, filtered or sieved and given him to drink. My mother often gave us a cough medicine known as Mndumbavathi. I have never been able to find the English word for it, possibly it isn't found beyond that part of Africa, so I can't give you the recipe! In this case, the leaves of this plant are chewed. It has a bitter taste and it makes the tongue numb. Another plant used to treat coughs is the *Mtango* — again I don't know the English translation. You chew the whole plant, leaves and stalk, with a pinch of salt. The taste is hard to describe, only that it, too, leaves the tongue numb. John was given some by my uncle, Mzee Zuberi, and he didn't like it at all!

When our children were growing their milk teeth, I must have already become "westernised," because I used a powder called "Ashton's," which I rubbed onto their gums. We were fortunate to have easy access to a pharmacy and a hospital when our children were small, and we did not have to rely on medicinal plants. Our children didn't have to put up with the bitter taste and the numb tongue, but who is to say whether they were any less effective than the commercial medicines I gave them.

Bedtime

There is no fixed time for babies or young children to go to bed. They are allowed to fall asleep on their mother's lap or on her back before they are taken to bed. There were no electronic baby monitors in our rural homes — although John tells me there were none when he was a child either! Children above the age of three go to bed when they are sleepy, even if they have to go to school the next day. There is no such thing as "adults' time." Adults and children spend the evening together, until everyone is ready for bed. Mothers generally go to bed at the same time as their children, often in the same bed. John and I shared a bed with each of our children in turn until they were a few months old. I slept between John and the baby. This meant that I had to take care not to roll onto the baby, I had to sleep facing them all night, without changing my position. When each child was about five months old, he or she then slept in a cot in our room. In the rural villages of Africa, like Usangi, we do not have cots or even know what they are, so many mothers sleep with their babies until they have stopped breastfeeding them.

TOILET TRAINING

When a toddler is no longer wearing nappies during the day, the mother will begin toilet training them. After their meal, she will take the toddler outside the house and sit on a three-legged stool, or on the ground with her legs stretched out in front of her. On the ground between her legs, she places a piece of old cloth, or a banana leaf, sits the toddler on her legs, and the child opens their bowels onto it. If the child grows restless, the mother distracts them by drawing their attention to whatever is going on around them. There may be chickens scratching, cats strolling around being cats, birds — anything to encourage the child to sit still. Fortunately, there is usually a lot going on around an African house! When the toddler has "performed," the mother will wipe or wash them. The soiled cloth is thrown into the toilet. We did not have "potties" like they do in England. So African mothers used a different toilet training technique, which we all probably learnt from our mothers. The toilet of an African house is usually situated outside and consists of a deep, often uncovered hole in the ground, far too dangerous for a tiny child to use. When the child is about four or five, the mother digs a hole in the ground at a distance from the family compound, especially for their use. Once the child has finished, mother will cover the hole with soil. Instant compost — an eco-friendly toilet!

In most African villages, the toilets are separate buildings with walls of straw for privacy, outside and well away from the main house. Usually there are separate toilets for men and women. These toilets do not have a seat, you have to squat to use them, which can be pretty uncomfortable for the elderly.

They are particularly not easy to use if you are wearing trousers, although when I was young it was very rare to see a village woman wearing trousers. Even today, women don't usually wear them. When one of my English female friends visited Tanzania, she often wore jeans. I had to explain that the best thing to do was take them off completely, then she could squat. She had imagined having to confront all kinds of challenges in her first trip to Africa, but not the toilet!

CHILDREN AT WORK AND PLAY

English children often go to bed with their favourite toys or some other treasured possession to cuddle and comfort them. When I was a child few rural families had toys. There were none for sale in the village shop; it was something people never thought of. Even those parents who did know about toys had other priorities — food and clothes, for instance. There was no money for luxuries like toys. We spent our days barefoot, and even went to school without shoes. Toys were just not part of our culture. The first thing I remember playing with was a maize cob, when I was about six and in primary school. I had an old piece of cloth which I wrapped around the cob, and that was my doll.

By the time children reached the age of five, they were expected to help with suitable work around the house. They helped the adults with the housework, or accompanied them to the river to fetch water. With a broom made of twigs, they would sweep the house, or they were ordered to keep an eye on their younger siblings. At five, a girl child was considered old enough to carry a baby, which their mother tied onto her back for her. When she reached the age of seven or eight, she would start helping to collect firewood from the nearby forests — always accompanied by an adult. At ten and above, girls were shown how to pound maize and how to cook, and they were also expected to help with the digging and weeding. Boys had an easier time of it than their sisters. While the girls laboured over the heavier tasks, boys spent their days outside the compound, looking after the family's livestock — goats, sheep and cows - although cows would be grazed much further away and younger boys would always be accompanied by an adult, from whom they learnt.

Despite being a girl, at the age of ten and at primary school, I was often asked at weekends to take the goats and sheep out to look for grazing. One thing I remember vividly from that time is being stung so often by wasps; once, when I got stung on my eye, it was swollen for days afterwards. I hated going out with the livestock, I wanted to be with the other children in the village, not off on my own. Even now, when I go to visit my families in rural Kenya and Tanzania, I see that much of their daily life is not so different from the life I led. The animals still have to be taken out for grazing!

As children, we did have some time to play, during school holidays, after Friday prayers and on nights when there was a full moon. I really enjoyed our moonlit games, when we danced. We children would form circles, singing, clapping hands and dancing. We had no sources of music, so we sang our own music, *Kipare* and *Kiswahili* songs that were passed down to us by our parents and grandparents. When we did have spare time during the day, we would play games with marbles that could sometimes be bought in town on market days. We also had our own version of the English game, "five-stones", using little shiny pebbles. I liked that game very much, perhaps because I was so good at it.

Nowadays, the lives of children, both girls and boys, are generally easier. Most attend primary school, although they are still expected to help with the chores when they are at home. Again, more is expected of girls than boys. Parents – especially mothers - justify this with the argument that girls have to learn how to perform household tasks in preparation for marriage, as if boys would not eventually get married and not be expected to do any household chores. I remember one of John's fellow teachers announcing that he had decided to look for a wife because he needed someone to cook for him. I must admit, however, that my account does not apply to all boys and young men. I have an unmarried nephew, for example, who is a teacher and does all his own housework. But I know this will change once he gets married!

Although I was brought up as I have described, it was probably different for children in urban areas. Now, I have extended family members who work and live in towns and cities in Kenya and Tanzania. They employ someone to help with work in and around the house, often a young relative or someone from their home village, recruited through word-of-mouth recommendation. Even today, these "servants" (and that is what they are even if we do not like the word) are referred to as 'house-girls', who help in the house and 'house-boys', who do the outside chores such as cleaning the compound and washing the car.

Our children were lucky, because we could afford to buy some toys for them. Our son Mani always wanted a toy car to play with but he preferred the home-made cars to those bought in a shop. He had a friend called Martin, whose father worked in the same school as John and lived in our compound, who shared his passion for cars. Martin was special in Mani's eyes because he knew how to make his own toy cars, out of old tin cans cut up and bent to shape. The wheels of the cars were made by cutting circles from old flip-flops pushed onto sticks for axles — they really did turn round when the car was pushed along the ground. Martin was old enough to be allowed to use the scissors and even a knife to cut up the tin. I am sure most English parents would be horrified at the idea, but Martin was very adept and very sensible. His cars were a wonder to behold. They could be driven around by attaching a string or a stick, fitted with a "steering wheel." Even now, as an adult and a father in his own right, Mani still likes his cars.

First steps

When I was growing up in Kenya, women would encourage their babies to walk from the age of about nine months. The way they did this was by using a small homemade bell threaded on a string and tied around one of the toddler's ankles. The mother would then hold both of the toddler's hands to encourage walking and as the toddler walked, the tinkling of the bell, accompanied by assurances from the mother, would encourage the child to keep walking. The mother would also sing a song in *Kipare* language, 'Tete nana! Tete nana! *Uneveiwa*' ('keep walking! Keep walking! You can do it!'), while smiling at the child. I used this technique and the song with all my children. Tuni our eldest daughter was walking comfortably before she was ten months old but of course all children are different and some take longer than others.

Earrings

When I was about six years old I had my ears pierced, and it was very painful. I was asked beforehand if I wanted to have them pierced. Why did I say, "Yes" if it was going to hurt so much? I think now that at that age, I saw having my ears pierced as just part of growing up. Most of the older girls in the village had their ears pierced and wore earrings that I thought looked very pretty. I wanted to look pretty too and also I did not want to be different from the others. But also, I didn't realize just how much it would hurt!

A long thorn from an acacia tree was used to make the holes in my earlobes. Back then, we were not offered any other option. After my ears had been pierced, a length of cotton was threaded through the holes and tied in a loop so that they wouldn't close up. You may think this sounds very unhygienic and invited infection. Sometimes earlobes did get infected but with careful washing with soap and warm water until they had healed, there was usually no long-term problem. Until they had healed I did not wear any earrings, only wearing them much later, when my family could afford them.

When I came to England I was amazed to see shops where ears were pierced painlessly, using a cream to numb the earlobe and a "gun." Both our daughters had their ears pierced in England, and had their stud earrings inserted there and then. Thorns or needles are still commonly used in Kenyan and Tanzanian villages, although painless ear-piercing is available in the towns and cities. I was also very surprised, even shocked, to see men in England wearing earrings. Earrings are a 'girl thing' and a young man with an earring would be really frowned upon in East Africa.

Sleeping arrangements

Because African families tend to be quite large, finding spaces for everyone to sleep when there is a big family 'event' such as a wedding or a funeral can be a problem.

Sharing beds may then become the only option. In my experience, in Africa, men can share a bed together, but only if there is no other place to sleep, and they will remain almost fully clothed. There are some rules about this, however, although these are usually unspoken rules. For example, a grown-up son generally would not share a bed with his father, unless there really is no alternative.

Women, on the other hand, often sleep with other women, and not only in exceptional circumstances. I grew up sharing a bed with other girls, and I enjoyed it. Bedtime was the only opportunity we had to tell each other stories, or to exchange village gossip. We could relax with each other without the grown-ups listening in. The rest of the day was spent working; tilling the land, milking cows, grazing the livestock, collecting firewood, fetching water… the list was endless! But bedtime was a special 'us' time.

DRESSING CODES

When I was growing up, villagers had strong expectations of how people should dress, especially but not exclusively, women and girls. Women were supposed to wear skirts or dresses that covered their knees, and they should not wear trousers. Bare shoulders were not to be shown and if a woman raises her arm she should not expose her armpits or her bra, so sleeves were always cut to an appropriate length. I grew up in a Muslim family and there were other rules, although these were by no means as strict as those found in the Middle East. For one thing, I did not have to cover my head and face, which meant I could plait my hair and display it! Women were usually seen wearing a *lesso* or two wrapped around their waist or loosely thrown over their head and shoulders. These did cover most of a woman's body but more importantly it had the very practical purpose of protecting our dresses or other clothes from dirt or spillages when we were cooking or doing other jobs – such as milking the cows or digging in the farm. They also protected us from the direct heat of the sun.

Our madarasa teacher would remind us of this 'dress code' and the adults in my family agreed with him. They explained to us that women should dress modestly to protect the men from temptation. I learnt that, apparently, even the sight of the lower part of a girl's legs can inflame men's passions! On the other hand, men and young boys can wear more or less what they want, although only very young boys wear shorts. It seemed to me then as a young girl that it is only men who experience temptation and not women - or maybe women are expected to suppress their feelings.

Wapare women, and possibly others too, are not supposed to hang their washed underwear out to dry where men might see them. Only the husband is permitted to see a woman's underwear. Men, of course, can hang whatever item of clothing they like outside the house – or, in practice, their wives can wash them and hang them out. One rule for men and another for women.

Courtesy

Africans tend to respect a well-dressed person. A man who wears a suit and tie is shown more respect than someone dressed casually — they might even be greeted with a bow! Once, John had to go to Nairobi with his headmaster for a school meeting. A high-ranking official from the Ministry of Education put in an appearance. Afterwards, he shook hands with John's headmaster but refused to greet John. He turned to the headmaster and said, "Who is this man, dressed as if he is going to the beach?" John was certainly not dressed in shorts and a T-shirt, he was wearing his best formal shirt and trousers. In those days he just didn't happen to own a tie. The headmaster tried to excuse John by saying, 'On the coast it is very hot and therefore we tend to dress this way,' but the man still refused to talk to John. It's a shame that some people judge others by how they are dressed; they are not judged for what sort of people they are, but only on their appearance.

So, those who cannot afford to look 'smart' may be looked down upon, sometimes with an assumption that they are scroungers or thieves, even though they could be genuinely lovely people, and vice versa. When I was living in Mombasa, I was robbed by a man who was not only well dressed but also spoke very good English. Perhaps naively, I could not imagine he could be a thief, but a thief and a conman he was. I have written about this incident in my first book. Even Customs and Immigration officials seem to discriminate on the basis of appearance. Once I was crossing the border between Kenya and Tanzania, when an old lady in the queue just in front of me had a problem with her ID. Like most of the others in the queue, she wasn't particularly smartly dressed, nor were her clothes very clean. The officer at the border post was quite rude to her. When it came to my turn, I showed this officer my British passport and he asked me where I was going. I told him I was going to Moshi for a week to see my family. He asked me if I had been to Moshi before, and I replied, "Yes many, many times". He stamped my passport and gave it back to me, smiling and saying politely, "*Karibu Tanzania*", meaning 'welcome to Tanzania'. I cannot be sure whether he treated me differently from the old lady because I had a British passport or because I was more smartly dressed than she was.

On another occasion at the Tanzania border I did have a problem with an immigration official even though I was dressed smartly! Looking me up and down, she asked me where I had got a British passport from, to which I replied, "I find your question rather disturbing, because you are judging me, assuming that someone like me could not have a British Passport!" She huffed a bit, and said, "Well, with your accent I now know you are not a local person." She stamped my passport, gave me a wooden smile, and waved me on. When some Africans are given a bit of power, they take it as a license to be rude to ordinary people. It makes me ashamed to say that and it shouldn't be this way. I put it down to a general lack of education. It's harder to educate those who think that they are already better than others. Now that I have travelled much more, I realise that it is not just Africans who can behave like this. I have experienced this sort of attitude and behaviour in many other countries. I hope that one day, people will learn that treating others with respect isn't a sign of weakness, but of strength.

The entry desk at Nairobi Airport appeared to have been deliberately designed so that the officer sitting behind it looked down on the passengers arriving. Being short, I was forced to stand on tiptoe and stretch to hand over my passport whenever I entered Kenya from England. It felt demeaning and emphasised the power difference between the officer and me. The officer's facial expression and way of addressing me, made me feel even more uncomfortable and unwelcome. I think other people must have complained about this because when I arrived a few years later I found that the desk was at a reasonable height and, if anything, it was me who looked down on the officer. The tables had been turned – literally! The officials, too, are much more polite and welcoming these days. Politeness costs nothing.

A video on social media sent to me by a former schoolfriend showed a poorly-dressed man driving an old car being stopped by the Kenyan traffic police. They searched the man and his car, opening the boot and rummaging through his possessions. They even checked the spare tyre. Finding nothing, they waved the now very angry man away.

As he continued with his journey, the man had an idea. He would re-do the journey, this time dressed smartly and driving a newer car. He told the friend he had been going to see about the incident. His friend told him to forget it, but he was determined to carry out his plan. He drove home using a different route, avoiding the police checkpoint. When he arrived home, he had a shower and put on a suit and tie. Picking up a gun he owned, he got into his second, newer car and headed for the checkpoint where he had been stopped. The same policeman was still on duty, and seeing the smart car, waved the man through, just as he had expected. He brought his car to a halt and reversed up to the policeman and said to him, "I was driving an old car through your checkpoint a few hours ago. You stopped me and gave me a hard time. Now I am dressed smartly and driving a brand new car, and you wave me through! The first time, when I looked shabby, I had nothing on me. Now I look smart I am carrying a gun!" He indicated the gun lying on the passenger seat beside him. This video was circulated widely on social media. It is very likely of course that the video used actors rather than being a real-life incident, but the point is that the filmmaker wanted to show the sort of experiences that he and others have had with the police. What is sad is that none of us who watched the video was at all surprised by the story it told. This is how life is in Kenya; dress smartly and you can potentially get away with murder!

My next story I know to be true, as several friends and family members independently witnessed it. Two men from Taveta town wanted to raise money for their local primary school. Each had a woven basket for people to put their donations in, and they also had a loud hailer. One man was dressed smartly in a suit and tie, while the other wore clothes that were more casual. They took up their positions at a distance from each other, so as to cover more people in the market. They agreed to meet again in three hours and see how much they had raised. In an hour, the man in a suit and tie had already collected a lot of money — all in notes — while all the casually dressed man had in his basket was a few coins. Once again, people judged others according to their appearance. I wonder if this is just an African tendency, or is it more widespread?

Women in trousers

My experience in Kenya and Tanzania of women wearing trousers was and still is, that it is frowned upon, almost being a taboo. In the villages of my youth I never once saw a woman in trousers. The effect of this was that, at the time, I believed that trousers were only for men. In my culture and other cultures that I know of in Kenya and Tanzania, women themselves would never think of wearing trousers, just as their parents and grandparents before them would have thought. A woman wearing trousers, was not just disapproved of but unimaginable. In a way, it made sense because skirts and dresses are much cooler in the hot climate. It also made going to the toilet a whole lot easier, given that you have to squat. I am yet to find out how men manage!

I my rural family now have modern toilets, with seats. Nevertheless, women who wear trousers are still frowned upon, especially if the trousers are tight. They are regarded as being "loose women". Even some young men do not like being seen with a woman in trousers. I suppose they think it reflects badly on them. In 1988, John and I and our children went to visit our relatives in Kenya and Tanzania. Our daughter Tuni, then almost thirteen, wore trousers to visit my mother, who lived in the village of Kirongaya. On our way, we met with a lady, who when she saw Tuni stopped in astonishment. Why was my daughter wearing trousers like a boy? "Do you wish she was a boy?" she said. I explained that where we live, it is common for trousers to be worn by both boys and girls. What country was that, she asked, shocked to hear such a country existed. Then, shaking her head in bemusement, she said, "*Haya*" (okay) and walked away. I don't know what she really thought of us. Because she had never before seen a girl or a woman wearing trousers, she felt she had to ask me about it. I have a feeling my answer didn't make much sense to her. Maybe she had not been very far from the village in her life and all she knew was that: 'Trousers are for men!'

I totally understood the lady's reaction. When I was living in the village, I too believed that trousers were only for men. It wasn't until I went to Mombasa, in 1978, that I saw girls wearing trousers. Like the lady in Kirongaya, I was quite horrified. Even there, many women believed that women in trousers were "loose." Only when I had been living in Mombasa for a few years did I realise that this was not always the case. As for me, I only dared to put on a pair of trousers when we were in England in 1984. I thought I was safe then, because none of my family or friends would see me, although it was also the first time for our children to see me in trousers. I realised it was sensible to wear trousers in the aeroplane and certainly to wear them in England in December, because they kept me warmer. I was now making a decision about what to wear based on what was 'sensible' rather than on cultural expectations. Now I wear trousers almost every day, but when I go back to my home village, I make sure to wear a skirt, so as not to offend my family. They would stare and whisper or they would more probably give me a pair of *lessos* to cover my legs. I can just imagine their comments if I did not wear the *lessos*: "An old woman like you, why are you wearing trousers? What are you after at your age?"

How would you answer such questions? The best thing for me might be to walk away, because they have already judged me and it would better to ignore them to stop any conflict. They don't mean to be nasty, it is just how they have been brought up, possibly having lived in the same villages all their lives and followed the same dress code.

THERE IS STILL TIME TO DANCE

People in the village where I was brought up worked hard, toiling on the land. We knew of no other way to live. Still, there was time in the evening to tell stories, in bed or after our supper. Adults and children went to bed when they felt like it. There was no set "bedtime" like there is for many families in Britain. When the moon was full, we could go outside, and spend the evening singing and dancing. Someone who has spent most of their life in a developed country, where everyone relies on street lights, may not appreciate just how much light the moon, and the stars, provides. On clear nights we practised our traditional dances — keeping an eye open for Mr Bakari, if he was at home, who thought dancing was a waste of time. Mr Bakari thought we should concentrate on schoolwork instead of frivolous pursuits like dancing. Luckily, he was working in Dar-es-Salaam at the time, only coming to the village every four to five months, so we used the opportunity to entertain ourselves after a hard day's work. Not all heads of households were so strict, it varied from one family to another.

In the village of Kitoghoto, we girls would dress up in beads of different colours wrapped around our waists, and a wreath of more beads around our heads. The young boys would beat on the drums while we girls danced in a circle around them, moving our hips to the rhythm of the beat. There were always a few adults present, who would observe us and correct our dancing if we deviated from traditional moves, preparing us to carry on this important aspect of our culture in future generations. This was part of the preparation of young girls for their future adult life. In *Kipare* we call this preparation of girls, 'kuekwa'.

The equivalent preparation for the boys takes place when they are a bit older, when they are already 'young men'. It is called *Mshitu*. The older men take the young men into the forest away from the village, for several days. There, they are taught secret cultural traditions and practices. I have no idea what they are actually taught because it really must remain secret and no Pare man will ever discuss '*Mshitu*' with a woman, not even with his wife. It is a form of initiation into adulthood. Western religion and schooling have done much to suppress these practices, but they still take place, even today.

I will never forget those nights of dancing. While we danced to the rhythm of the drums, the beads around our waists swung from side to side, their colours flashing in the moonlight. I often wish my children could have had such experiences of Pare traditional dancing in the moonlight. I still enjoy dancing at home, as long as there is no one watching - apart from our grandchildren who I have been encouraging to move their hips in time to African music. It is not really the same as learning my traditional dances but it is good for them to maintain a connection, however tenuous, with their African traditions and roots. Farida and Jeremy's children, who are younger than their cousins, will dance without any shyness. Tuni and Simon's son, Zain used to dance both African and what he told me are Welsh styles, because his father is Welsh. Now Zain is much older he is too shy to dance and would rather focus on his football.

DOING THE LAUNDRY

During my childhood in the village of Eldoro, weekends were spent doing extra household chores and collecting firewood, on top of the usual weekday tasks. We washed our clothes by hand using water from the river, though not in the river, because it was also our source of drinking water. We took buckets and plastic bowls with us to the river, and bars of soap which tended to make our hands dry when we used it to wash clothes. Although soap powder was available in the Taveta town shops, only much later could we afford to buy it. When we got to the river, we filled the buckets and bowls with water and washed our clothes, along with those of the very old and the very young family members, on the river bank. We would then spread them out to dry on the grass or on bushes by the river. That way, they weren't so heavy to carry home. Since it was usually warm and sunny, we did not have long to wait before the clothes were dry. If the clothes were very dirty or stained, they would have to be soaked first before being scrubbed by hand or with a brush.

The river carried the disease bilharzia (or schistosomiasis). This is caused by parasites from snails that live in still water and enter the body through the skin.

It isn't necessary to drink the water to catch bilharzia, just coming in contact with it can be enough. Most people in Eldoro would have caught bilharzia at some time in their lives. The symptoms include chronic fatigue, and blood in the urine. It can be treated, but because the river is the only source of water, people catch the disease again and again. I had it numerous times. It is a very unpleasant thing to have! I was suffering from bilharzia when I arrived in England, and naturally, my GP couldn't diagnose it. Eventually I told him I needed to be seen by a specialist in tropical diseases, who diagnosed bilharzia. I was given tablets that had been made especially for me. I was told I was lucky to be a British citizen, otherwise I would have been obliged to go to back to Kenya for treatment.

No one in the village had a washing machine. In those days we did not know such machines existed and anyway, there was no electricity supply. Nowadays some of the people who live in towns and cities, like my niece Zania, do use washing machines, but many still wash their clothes by hand. So do the majority of people who are still in the villages I know, although they no longer use the river. The people in the village of Eldoro now have clean running water from a deep borehole. Most of the streams and rivers have a bridge over them, so no one has to walk through bilharzia-infected water.

Holidays

We usually spent most of our school holidays working on the farm. The thought of going away on a holiday never even crossed our minds. The miserable weather in Britain causes most people to wish to go on a holiday that includes sunshine, beaches and swimming. In East Africa, the sun is almost always shining and there is a long coastline with beautiful beaches, but people tend to use what free time they have to visit family and friends as a break from their routine. For those who do visit the coast, going swimming is a possibility that many may enjoy but – when I was younger – Muslim women would not usually be included in swimming unless they were fully-clothed. Muslim women are forbidden to expose any part of their body to strangers, especially men. In contrast, men don't have to be fully clothed. I assume this is because they think that women will not be tempted by the sight of a partially clothed man's body! If women do have any such temptations, we are supposed to suppress our feelings and not talk openly about men.

I was brought up in a large family where holidays were beyond our means. There was only one person in paid employment, Mr Bakari, whose salary was barely enough to feed everyone. We all had to work very hard from a young age to supplement the money he earned by growing much of our food – we ate 'by the sweat of our brows'. Most of the people in the village did not go on holiday either, but we didn't miss holidays because we had no experience of them.

READING AND BOOKS

I enjoyed primary school very much, partly because it was an escape from household chores and farm work. We only had textbooks at school, which we read only to pass exams, apart from a few storybooks which we read in class, or which the teacher read to us. Most of these books were written in *Kiswahili*. We did not have a school library, indeed we didn't know what a library was until we got to secondary school. Reading anything other than textbooks was just not something we were used to doing. Also, reading took time, which was something we didn't have, what with all the work we had to do. Reading for pleasure would have been seen as a waste of time — if it had ever happened. On the rare occasions when we read at home it would be a textbook that I had brought home to help me prepare for an exam. Having said that, there was one small storybook in our home. This was a book written in the *Kipare* language, with the title *Kireri uthimutheke Iraro,* which literally translates as "a young banana bud should not mock the old leaves." The moral of the story told in this book was that young people should not make fun of old people, because those old people were once young themselves. The only other books I remember were a handful of religious books in the *Madrasa,* which were compulsory reading. I would say that reading is not part of our culture. For the very poor, books are a luxury, and many people are illiterate. When I told my extended family members in Kenya and Tanzania that I had written a book about my life, their response was unenthusiastic. Anyway, they said, they could not afford to buy the book . Ordinary families would rather spend the money on more important things, such as feeding and clothing the family. Some, especially those in Tanzania, reminded me that they can't understand a book written in English. Perhaps I should have written in *Kiswahili* or even my mother tongue, *Kipare*?

Most of the Africans I know would rather spend their spare time sitting chatting with friends or family rather than reading. In the past, when I was a child, many girls received no education at all. I was the first girl from the village of Eldoro to go to secondary school, thanks to the support of my father and, later, Mr Bakari, who stepped in to help me with the school fees. At that time, my father could not afford the school fees, particularly because he had been forced to stop doing his tailoring job because of his poor eyesight.

GAMES

I enjoyed games very much when I was at school, and I was good at them too. Taking part in games of hopscotch, skipping and netball were some of the best times in my early life. Some of the teachers liked me because I was both good in class and good in sports. I continued to enjoy sports such as netball and running when I was at secondary school. I enjoyed competing with other children of my age, because I was confident of winning. The praise I received made me want to go on and do more. I was a very competitive student! Our daughter Tuni's children are also very competitive. I remember when our granddaughter Savannah was chosen to compete in the running in her school's sports day and John wished her all the best, she answered with a confident, "I expect to win!" And she did. She can even be disappointed if she comes second. Farida's children are also competitive, especially Sahara, the youngest. Her self-confident attitude has led us to call her, lovingly, "Madam Sahara."

DEATH AND FUNERALS

In Islam, someone who dies has to be buried the very next day. In African rural areas, they will usually be buried within the family compound. I am not sure what happens in big towns and cities. Muslim burials are different from those of other faiths, where the bodies are interred in a churchyard or cemetery. The men, wearing a white turban or the traditional Muslim *kofia,* dig the grave. While they are digging the grave, the women of the village gather in the house, comforting the bereaved family.

The women attending the funeral are expected to wear a long dress or a pair of *lesso,* and must cover their heads. The family of the deceased continue to wear long, dark dresses and for weeks after the funeral.

Before the burial, the deceased's body is washed and carefully wrapped in a shroud, always being handled with great respect. Women are washed by women, and men by men. This washing of the body was and still is the only part of the funeral in which women participate. The men take care of the actual placing of the body in the grave. (The only exception to this rule that I have come across was when a very young baby died a long way from the parents' home and was buried by the mother. In that instance, it was against the law to transport a dead body in public transport, the father was far away at home and the mother could not afford to hire a vehicle.) Thus, I have never seen an open grave and I only learned much later that when the grave is prepared, a little chamber is dug at one end for the head. The head should always remain uncovered while the rest of the body is being covered with soil. The body is always buried with the head facing Mecca, the Holy City and the most important place in Islam.

In Kenya and Tanzania, when someone dies, there is a lot of loud weeping and wailing. This is partly a way of announcing the death to others. (Loud crying can, of course, also signal that a woman is being beaten by her husband! However, wife-beating rarely occurred in the villages I lived in.) Someone from the village (usually a couple of men) will go to find out why there was a big cry. If there has been a death, practically the whole village will gather at the home of the grieving family. They will bring food, water and firewood, and the women villagers will set about preparing food for the family and mourners. In this practical way, they are expressing their sympathy with the family. Some will stay with the deceased's family for nearly a week, bringing their own mats to sleep on.

The dead person will be laid out on a bed and covered with a sheet. Those who want to pay their last respects will go into the room to see the body for the last time and utter some respectful words. As far as I can remember, children are not usually encouraged to view the body.

I was surprised to find that people in England are so quiet following a death. When John's father died, I cried loudly, and was asked not to. This is one of many cultural differences that I have had to learn about over the years. I really can't say that any one culture is better than any other. Indeed, differences are to be welcomed and respected, although there are, of course, limits to what is permitted in the name of "our culture."

A friend and colleague of mine who was a Health Care Assistant originally from West Africa told me that in her grandmother's time, a husband and wife were always buried together. If the wife died years after her husband, he would be dug up and his remains arranged on top of his wife's dead body, which was lying in a coffin. The coffin containing the two of them would then be buried in the husband's grave. At the graveside the family sings a song in praise of the reunion of the couple, and the good memories they have left behind with the family. After the funeral, people eat and drink and remember all the good things that happened in the couple's lives. After that, someone would lead a prayer for the dead before everyone went home.

When John and I were living in China, I learned that the Tibetan people have many different types of funeral. These include burial and cremation, but the funeral practice that I find particularly interesting - though strange - is the "sky burial". This entails taking the body to a designated site in the mountains, where it is left for the vultures to feed on, having first been chopped into pieces. I must admit that when I first heard of this I shuddered at it. It seemed disrespectful to the deceased person, especially the chopping-up bit. Then, I thought about it, and came to see the ecological aspect of dealing with bodies this way, even though this may not be the reason behind the practice. Even cremation is something I am not sure about. My parents and all my aunts and uncles were buried after their death and whenever I go back to Kenya and

Tanzania, I like to take visit their graves and place flowers there while remembering the time I spent with them. Graves give me special places in which to do this and to be "with" my deceased loved ones.

My aunt Khadija told me that when she was young, it was the practice among *Wapare* families to bury their deceased loved ones in one of the bedrooms of the family home. The body would be buried standing or sitting upright, with the head sticking out above the surface of the soil when the grave was filled. This room would be securely shut and regular checks to see if the head had dropped off. When this was seen to have happened, the family would vacate the house, which was then locked from the outside. The dead body would remain in that house until the building collapsed. In my aunt's time houses were simple mud and thatch dwellings, which soon disintegrated. The family would then move to a different house; some families would have more than just one house in the compound and so this was not difficult. This kind of burial is no longer practised, at least partly because it is not practical to move house whenever someone dies. For one thing, you lose a lot of land!

ENTERTAINING GUESTS

The *Wapare* are a hospitable people. Visitors are always made welcome; received with a big smile, repeated declarations of "*karibu*!"' (welcome) and a hug or a handshake. (Displays of body contact between men and women is discouraged amongst the *Wapare*.) The visitors are ushered into the sitting room and invited to take a seat.

If they have come a long way, the hosts will say *"pole."* This is an interesting word as it is widely used and has several levels of meaning. *Pole* expresses sympathy in any situation; it is said to anyone who has lost a loved one, or because a loved one is sick, or if a person falls down and hurts themselves, or to a traveller who is tired, and so on. Perhaps it is similar to the way English people say "Sorry" in all sorts of situations.

Once the guest has settled, he or she is then served *chai* (tea). Unlike in England, they are not first asked whether they would like some, probably because the offer would be refused out of politeness. After all, who would say no to a cup of *chai* after a long journey! So the host will simply say to the guest, "Please relax, I am going to make you *chai*." While the host goes off to make tea, the visitor remains with at least one host family member to keep them company. If there is no one to stay with the visitor, the host will take them with her since it is not polite to leave the visitor alone. Once the *chai* is ready, host and visitor return to the sitting room to drink it. If the guest was expected, or perhaps comes from another country, there might be some African-style doughnuts (*mandazi*) to go with the tea. The first cup is given to the guest, with a *"karibu sana"* (welcome). The host will enquire about their journey, and whether their family is well. After a while, they might go and sit outside and chat with other members of the family, and the children will all come forward to be introduced. We *Wapare* tend to talk a lot and tell long stories involving lots of laughter! When the time comes for the evening meal, if the guest is a woman, she will eat with the women, a man with the men, since women and men eat separately.

Children under five will sit with the women, while older boys will sit with the men.

The meal might consist of chapattis, served with chicken stew, or beef or kidney beans. Offering *mandazi* and chapattis shows that the visitor is valued, because making them is hard work and they take longer to cook than rice. There is no dessert; instead the visitor is offered local fruits, which may be bananas, pawpaw, or pineapples from the farm.

Traditionally, at least – and still very much so today - Africans tend to use their bare hands to eat, although sometimes it depends on the sort of food. It is always the right hand that is used for eating, never the left; children are taught this from a very early age, as soon as they start to eat with others. We therefore have to wash our hands thoroughly before and after eating. Hands are washed when everyone is seated at the table. One of the younger members of the family takes a bowl of water, soap and a towel to each person in turn, for them to wash their hands. The soap is rinsed off with water from a jug, poured by the same family member. Hands are washed in order of seniority — eldest first (unless there are guests) to youngest. When I was a child, we did not use a jug or soap and everyone washed and their hands in the same water. This meant that the water in the bowl grew progressively more dirty as it went round. Still, people survived — including me!

SOME TABLE MANNERS

People never blow the ir nose at the table and children are taught this from a very early age. If you need to do so, you must leave the table and then wash your hands before re-joining the others. No one must touch any other part of their body while eating with their hands, unless you are eating by yourself. Belching, however, is allowed, even encouraged, as it indicates that you have enjoyed your food. Our daughter, Tuni, was shocked to hear my aunt Khadija belching loudly and repeatedly, so she quietly decided to move away from the table as she was not accustomed to my culture.

HONOURED GUESTS

If a guest is considered really special, a cow may be slaughtered in honour of the occasion. This happened when John came to visit my family in Eldoro after we were married. Pili, a relative who had never seen a white person close to, turned up to have a look at this strange phenomenon. As is the custom, she greeted everyone in turn until she got to John. She stared at him for several seconds before turning to me and saying, "Can he eat *sima*?" *Sima* is the staple food of our people, consisting of maize meal cooked until it is stiff — rather like a cake — and can be eaten with the hand. I was puzzled at her question. When I asked Pili what she meant, she said she thought all white people had plastic teeth! She thought that these teeth must be delicate and could only be used to eat very soft meals. She went on to comment about how white he was. "Is his private part white too?" she asked. I didn't quite know how to respond! Mr. Bakari's wife heard Pili asking me these questions and retorted, "You are a black person, is your private part black?" I thought this was a very good way of dealing with Pili's strange question without actually answering it. Pili did not know what to say, so she was told to think for herself.

I was reminded of this kind of personal comment and question much later when I was living in China. Some Chinese people, too, can be very direct, asking all sorts of personal questions that I would consider rude. I certainly don't think they meant to be rude. It is just a cultural difference, but perhaps – as with Pili's questions – a degree of ignorance of the wider world plays a part too.

ADVICE FOR A NEW WIFE

When I was growing up, I was given a lot of advice as to how I should treat my future husband. First, I must never forget that he is the head of the family, and my duty is to serve him. I must make sure he eats well, giving him the biggest portion of food, and always serving him first. Men, I was told, always eat faster than women, so I should keep an eye on my husband's plate, in case it is empty. If it is, I must help him to more. When he has finished eating, I must help him to wash his hands and rinse them for him with water from a jug, after which he will shake them dry as we did not have towels in those days (using an 'all-purpose' *lesso* only after bathing). He is expected to show appreciation by saying "Asante" (thank you) for the meal and for helping him to wash his hands. And, of course, he never helps to clear the plates from the table. As for washing up… unthinkable!

I have observed that things may be changing and this may be a result in part of changes in houses, rather than in people's attitudes. At my niece's house in Moshi, there is running water and a sink with a towel hung next to it. She does not bring a bowl and towel to her husband or a visitor; it is simply more convenient if they use the sink. But, even today, much else remains the same; cooking, serving, washing up and all housework remain my niece's responsibility.

So, what does the husband do in return? Well, his first responsibility is to father children. Then he must provide for them. He must make sure there is enough food, and that the children go to school — if he can afford it. He must work on the farm. So must his wife, although he will probably be expected to do more. Some farm jobs, such as tending the livestock, are considered to be the responsibility of the men of the household. In order to pay for the children's education, he might decide to sell some of the farm produce in the market, although it is more often the women who actually do the selling. If there is an urgent need for money, some of the livestock may be sold, which is the husband's responsibility.

If he is a caring husband, particularly if he is well-off, he will employ a "house-girl" or a "boy" to help his wife. If he cannot afford to pay a servant, his wife will just have to do all the chores herself, until her children are old enough to give her a helping hand. When the new wife reaches this stage where there are others available in the house to help with the tasks that she has been expected to do, she can now allocate tasks to others. She now takes on a responsibility to ensure that all the work is done, and done well. Her husband will still be the 'boss' but he will expect his wife to ensure that work in the house – and on the farm – is managed correctly.

A WOMAN'S WORK IS NEVER DONE

My experiences in the villages I have lived in is that women have so many responsibilities, especially married women. My family being a Muslim family - everyone – men and women - got up very early in the morning, at about five o'clock for prayers. The first thing we did was to wash and then go for prayers (except for any woman who is menstruating). After prayers, the girls and the boys under about 14 years old went to fetch water from the river, which was about a fifteen-minute walk each way. This meant carrying a bucket or a pot of water on our heads, the way we had been brought to carry things. On our return from the river, there was milking the cows to be done. This was a job for the women or young girls. After milking, it was also the job of a woman or girl again to make '*chai*' for the whole family. Then we all sat down together and had breakfast. In my family, we very rarely had bread with *chai*, but we drank it with whatever food was left over from the previous night after warming it up. Very rarely, in my experience, would men or boys make the tea if there was a woman around.

After breakfast, everyone except those women tasked with looking after the younger children goes to the farm to till the land, or plant, weed or harvest the crops — maize, kidney beans, cabbages, and so on. The men and older boys go off first, leaving the women to clear up and wash the dishes. After labouring on the farm, the women and older girls collect firewood on their way home. They usually get home at around three o'clock, when they will have a late lunch, prepared by whoever stayed behind to take care of the children. We didn't usually take food with us to the farm, but would pick fruit and cut sugar cane to hold our hunger until we got back home. After lunch, the women prepare supper for the family. They then have to milk the cows again. By the end of the evening the women are exhausted. They relax and chat until they feel ready for bed, which can be any time. There is no set bed time, even for young children. We went to bed when we were tired. Every day follows the same routine, except for Friday, which is the Muslim holy day for prayers and rest. We rarely took holidays, but sometimes we would go to visit our friends and extended family members, which often meant a trip across the border into Tanzania.

MY FIRST HOLIDAY

Perhaps because holidays were unusual I still clearly remember my first proper holiday, when I was fifteen and I went to Dar-es-Salaam, then the capital of Tanzania, to visit Mr Bakari. His wife was living in the village, and she visited her husband every two to three months. On this occasion, Mrs Bakari invited me and her niece Safia to accompany her. Safia and I were thrilled, especially because we were going to see somewhere new. To us, it was like a dream come true. If you have read my first book, "A Tale for My Children and Grandchildren," you might remember Mr Bakari, and the history between me and him. We travelled to Dar by train. It was the first time I had ever been on a train and it was a long, long journey. We set off from Taveta town, on the Kenyan side of the border at midday, and did not arrive in Dar-es-Salaam until four o'clock the following afternoon. We travelled third class, on hard wooden seats, where the only source of ventilation — and dust — was the windows. The smell, a combination of sweat and the chickens that people carried with them in baskets as presents for those whom they were going to visit, was overpowering. Some people in our carriage became sick from the long journey, lack of comfort, and tiredness, and some were throwing up out of the open windows.

Progress was agonisingly slow. The train stopped at every single station, long enough for people to get on and off, but also to buy something to eat. Local people lifted up their products to the open windows, shouting "Ndizi, ndizi!" or "Mahindi ya kuchoma!", telling us they were selling bananas or roasted maize. Others climbed onboard to sell their food, not leaving until the train was already whistling its departure, at which point those passengers who had got out to stretch their legs were also rushing to get back onboard. Each departure was therefore a moment of chaos. We were offered ripe bananas, roasted cassava, roasted maize, boiled maize, chapatis and doughnuts, along with drinks such as Fanta, Coca-Cola and water. My favourite was the roasted maize. I have never forgotten that journey, even though it happened fifty years ago. Despite the smell and the endless stops, Safia and I were not put off in the slightest. We arrived in Dar-es-Salaam dripping with sweat but excited. Mr Bakari was waiting for us at the station. He herded us into a bus, our luggage stacked wherever we could find space inside or on the roof.

We stayed there for about three weeks, only going out to go shopping or to visit one of Mr Bakari's friends. We didn't think of going 'for a walk' or sightseeing. It was not a "holiday" as you might understand it and Mr Bakari's small house was hot and stuffy, but for all that, it made a welcome change.

While we were there, Mr Bakari took us to see a man who had magic that would give us protection against snakebite. Mr Bakari explained to us that, because we worked very hard in the farm and sometimes encountered snakes there, it was a good idea to have this African magic protection. The *mganga* (something between a traditional herbalist and a sorcerer) made a number of small cuts on our bodies with a razor, to which he applied a black paste resembling tarmac. Once he had finished, the *mganga* told us we were not to have a shower for three days. The very next day we took the train back to Taveta. Safia and I, covered in this black stuff, felt dirty, sticky and hot – and we could not wash for three days! At the time I don't think I really believed that the procedure would protect us from snake bites, but we could not challenge Mr Bakari. We did as we had been told and spent three days without washing. Since then, neither Safia nor I have ever been bitten by a snake. What would have happened if we hadn't had this "treatment"? I don't know. Do you?

When we were in Dar-es-Salaam, I saw my first person

with albinism. This man was a neighbour of Mr Bakari's. He was very pale, his hair was white and his eyes seemed to flutter constantly. Seeing this "white" man triggered the memory of the first time — when I was about six years old — I saw a white man and thought that I was seeing God. I have described this in my previous book.

When I was in secondary school, there was a girl two years below me who had pale skin and hazel eyes and hair that was lighter than ours. She was not an albino, though. Her family home was in Wundanyi, the administrative centre of Taita-Taveta District. She was a kind girl with a ready smile that made her popular with many students. I sometimes used to wonder why she was pale, but it did not really matter to us what shade her skin was, and no one said much about it. African skin colour does vary, from being very black, through shades of brown to being quite light. My mother was light-skinned, whereas my father and his siblings all had dark skins.

Unfortunately, albino people are often treated cruelly in Tanzania. Some have been killed and their body parts used in so-called traditional magic. It is an extreme and perverted form of racism. I have experienced racism, and so have my children, but I have learned to deal with it. I feel sorry for those people who resent others just for the way they look, because they miss out on so much. I like to think that having known so many different types of people I have come to realise just how unimportant outward appearances really are.

IN-LAWS

In the *Wapare* tribe it is not customary for a son-in-law to eat at the same table as his mother-in-law. The reason given for this is that a man must not see his mother-in-law chewing her food, and vice-versa. When Mr Bakari got married, he did not shake hands with his mother-in-law, and would keep some space between them both when greeting her. To me it looked as though was they were uncomfortable with each other, but it was just the way he had been brought up. Even when passing each other, they would keep some distance apart. I was reminded of this many years later, when we had to keep our distance during the COVID-19 pandemic. I am pleased to say that my mother did not behave in this way with her son-in-law. This wasn't because John isn't a *Mpare,* she was simply more modern in her outlook. My father was the same, and I am grateful to them both for being examples of tolerance and independent thinking.

GROWING UP

When I was growing up in the villages of Kitoghoto and Eldoro, women and children would eat their evening meal sitting on the floor, while the men and boys sat at the table. While women were eating, they would be chatting away about anything; it could be about the day they have had, or about someone they knew. People normally would not sit quietly while eating; there would be conversation and jokes and laughter. Children up to the age of about twelve were not allowed to participate in the conversations of their elders. They would be told, *"Wandu wabaha wekigaya uthiingilie,"* meaning "when adults are having a conversation don't interrupt and don't join in." This could not have been a cultural norm, however, since I knew other families where everyone joined in the conversations. I am sure that this had an effect on me. Even after I grew up, I was shy around people older than myself, but not my friends. For example, in 1978 when I was studying shorthand and typing in Mombasa, I arranged to meet John and some of his friends at the Manor Hotel for lunch and a drink. I was very quiet throughout, and would only speak in order to answer a question. I was brought up to believe children should be "seen but not heard," as the saying goes. A child could still have a conversation with an adult, but this was not encouraged when a group of adults were talking together.

You might say my upbringing was a mixture of two parts — the traditional and the modern. As I have written, my mother and father, with whom I lived until I was five, were more "modern" in their outlook, and even when I was small, they gave me quite a lot of freedom. In contrast, my aunt and her family were much more traditional, and with them I had to abide by much stricter rules. You might think I must be a confused mixture, and maybe I am! I was indeed often rather quiet and withdrawn when I first left home, away from the village and into the modern city life of Mombasa. When I began to travel more and meet people from different backgrounds and cultures I found, however, that I had the strength and confidence to fully engage with these new experiences and people. I am pretty sure it was the influence of my mother and father in my very early years that enabled me to do this, and I thank them wholeheartedly for it.

I can't quite believe how confident I have become. A while back, I was invited by BBC Radio Derby to be interviewed about my first book, "A *Tale for My Children and Grandchildren*." I was a bit nervous beforehand, and I even asked the presenter, Ian Skye, to send me some of the questions in advance so that I could prepare myself. He was so nice and told me not to worry, because it was going to be just a normal chat together with some music breaks. When I arrived at the studio, everyone was so nice and gave me big smiles, which did so much for my self-confidence. John came with me, and we were offered a drink, the atmosphere was very relaxed and the interview went well; I found I was not nervous after all. Our neighbours listened to it, and all said they thought I did very well, which was again a big boost to my confidence. Since then, I have had several invitations to give talks to the residents of Brassington, where John and I live. I can still hardly believe I did it – and in my third language too! The calico ("primitive") girl from rural villages in Tanzania and Kenya is now able to stand in front of people and talk about her life with confidence — I have even danced for them! I am amazed at myself and I give a very big "Thank you" to all those who have supported me.

DOCTORS AND HOSPITALS

In some African villages, such as Kitoghoto where I first went to live with my aunt Khadija, getting to see a doctor if one was unwell was difficult. There were no transport services; Kitoghoto was the most remote village I have ever lived in. The only means of transport was a bicycle, and not many people owned one. We went everywhere on foot. The nearest hospital was more than ten kilometres away: too far to walk if you are unwell. People had to rely on someone who had a bicycle to help transport the patient. We in the villages always cooperated and looked after each other, especially in difficult situations. If the patient was too weak to sit on a bicycle, he or she would have to be carried on a stretcher. It would take four young men to carry the stretcher, probably walking barefoot and at any time of day – in the heat of the day or at night, when torches had to be used to see their way and avoid treading on a snake.

In addition to the patient, the stretcher-bearers would have to carry water to drink. The water was kept cool in calabashes, which are almost as good as a thermos flask for this purpose. Progress was slow, as you can imagine, with the stretcher-bearers needing to take a break every so often, though not too often if the patient was very unwell. The patient also had to be kept hydrated with regular sips of water. If it was malaria, probably the commonest illness in these cases, they would need urgent treatment. This then was how the people of the village ran their own ambulance service!

On arrival at the hospital, they would have to queue to see the doctor. The hospital was always busy, and there was usually only one doctor on duty, perhaps supported by a Medical Officer. The doctor would record the patient's details on a card, including their age. This could be a difficult question for many patients, especially the older ones, who didn't know their date of birth.

Later, I lived in the village of Eldoro, which was still ten kilometres away from the hospital but did have a transport service — a mini-bus which passed the village twice a week, on market days. Agostino, who owned the village shop, also had a Land Rover, which greatly benefited the villagers when they needed emergency transport, such as for taking sick people to the hospital. Life in Eldoro was certainly a step up from Kitoghoto. The family of a patient in the hospital was (and still is) responsible for their care beyond their immediate medical needs, such as administering drugs. A family member has to stay at the bed-side to make sure the patient is comfortable. They have to provide food for their relative, and even water to drink. Unmarried female patients are looked after by the women of the family, male patients by the men, while those who are married can be looked after by their spouse. Care provided by the family includes washing and dressing the patient.

In 2013, my son Mani and I went to visit family in Kenya. While we were there, Mr Bakari became ill, so his wife, Mani and I took him to Taveta Hospital in a car belonging to another family member. I knew the doctor who examined Mr Bakari; we had both attended the same secondary school. Mr Bakari was admitted. We were given a wheelchair and took him to the ward. The nurse at the reception desk was chatting to her fellow nurses and paid no attention to us, so I asked her if we could get a bed for our patient. After waiting a while, she turned to us and asked Mani to take the patient to his bed, which she pointed out. I said, *"kijana wangu hajui Kiswahili,"* meaning "my son does not speak *Kiswahili.*" Curious, she asked Mani where he was from. I told her she should be paying attention to the patient - advice which did not go down well. Her reaction clearly showed she thought I should not have told her what to do. I said I was sorry, but she should be concerned about the patient rather than my son.

We took Mr Bakari to the bed, made him comfortable and his wife gave him a little wash. This was quite normal; even washing a patient or taking them to the toilet is not the nurses' responsibility. Family members have to stay with their sick relatives, sleeping in a chair by the bed. They remain there overnight and have to try to sleep on the hard, uncomfortable wooden chairs.

Later that day, I overheard the nurse complaining to a group of doctors that I had been rude to her. She said she had never been spoken to like that by any other member of a patient's family and, as a nurse, she did not expect to be spoken to in that way. What she did not know was that one of the doctors she was speaking to was my half-brother, and he related her comments to me.

Her behaviour had come as a shock to me, particularly because at the time I was working for the NHS as a Health Care Assistant. The patients were our responsibility, and we were expected to treat them with respect and consideration. I found the nurse's attitude disturbing. In 2013, hospital patients still had to be looked after by their relatives! Unbelievable. Many years earlier I had experienced nurses in Kenya being rude and seemingly uncaring when I had taken Mani to hospital at the age of just three months, but I had assumed - or maybe just hoped - that things would have changed since then. Sadly, I was wrong and I felt disappointed.

HOW OLD ARE YOU?

On one occasion when I was living in Eldoro, I accompanied a family member to the hospital. As usual, there was a long queue. At last, there was only an elderly man waiting in front of us. When he got to the desk, the doctor asked, "habari gani, bwana?" (how are you?). The man replied, *"mimi naumwa,"* ("I am not well"). The doctor then asked him for his name and his age. The man replied that he was ten years old. "Sorry?" the doctor said. "How old?" "Ten," the man said again. The doctor replied, "You look old enough to be my father, how can you be ten years old!", but the man insisted he was indeed ten years old. In the end the doctor simply wrote "adult" on the man's card. The doctor did not seem particularly surprised by this. Many people, especially those who hadn't been to school, had no birth certificate. Many, including me, were born at home and not at the hospital. I was unusual in that my father - being somewhat educated - recorded his children's dates of birth in an exercise book, which he kept. This meant that – unlike some of my contemporaries – I have always known my date of birth and, of course, my age. In Britain, it is taken for granted that everyone knows their date of birth – and they have to give it so often for a passport, driving licence, medical records, and so on. Without my father's record, I would have had to make up a date, like many people used to do in Kenya and Tanzania. In the "modern" society, that Kenya has now become, it is important to know your date of birth because it will be asked for in so many situations – going to school, getting a passport and even a local ID booklet, a driving licence, and so on.

When I was growing up, birthdays weren't celebrated. Your birthday was just another day, like any other, and no one ever wished me "Happy Birthday". Nowadays, some middle class educated Africans will celebrate their birthdays, but most do not, especially if they are living in rural villages. Knowing what date you were born does not mean you will celebrate your birthday. It wasn't ignorance which stopped us having birthday parties. Holding a birthday party is just not part of our culture.

Those people who do celebrate their birthdays don't send cards, which are considered a waste of money. But we might have a party - because everyone likes a party! A children's party is likely to resemble a British one, with a decorated cake, sweets and soft drinks, along with party games. For adults, the family will (if they can afford it) prepare a special meal of pilau — rice cooked with meat or chicken and spices. A birthday cake may be served for dessert, sometimes with fruit. Guests bring birthday presents — which they would do anyway, since no one visits empty-handed. Not everything we do now is copied from Europeans!

Schools

In the village where I lived with my aunt Khadija, there was a small school with only one classroom, built of mud with a thatched roof. This school did not have many pupils. To encourage more parents to send their children to school, a couple of the teachers decided to go round the village explaining the importance of education to parents with children of school-going age. Some parents agreed to send their children to the school, but only the boys, not the girls. The girls, they said, were needed at home, to help their mothers with the chores, and because they had to learn the skills they would need when they got married and become mothers themselves. Boys, on the other hand, could be spared. The boys or their parents also might aspire to employment in a paid job, perhaps in town, and would need some education. Furthermore, boys were expected to support their parents in their old age, but girls would get married and leave the family for that of their husband. And then there was the question of school fees, even though these were quite small for primary school. Educating a son would be an investment, whereas money spent on school fees for a girl would benefit her husband's family, not them. Those fathers who had been to school – such as my father - would be more likely to see the importance of schooling, even for girls; those without education would be less aware of its value.

This was my uncle Zuberi's reasoning when he decided to stop paying my primary school fees. His words were, "Now you can read and write, there is no need to carry on with schooling." Luckily for me, my father objected, so I was able to complete primary school after all. Later, Mr Bakari paid my secondary school fees, which changed my life for the better. Nowadays, not only are girls encouraged to go to school, primary schooling is compulsory for all children, boys and girls above a certain age.

In the past it was difficult for some parents to know when their children had reached school age if they didn't know their dates of birth. Because of this, a way for parents and teachers to judge whether a child is ready to go to school had to be found. Parents were advised by the teachers on the best way to do this. A parent should hold the child's right hand and gently stretch the child's arm over the top of the head to see if the child can touch the left ear. If they were able to do so, the child is ready to start school. I was myself tested for school readiness using the teacher's method, even though I knew my age. I did this, mainly for fun and not to be singled out.

Wardrobes and suitcases

When I was growing up we did not store our clothes in wardrobes. We hung a sisal rope across our bedroom from one corner of the room to the opposite corner, like an indoor washing line, and hung our clothes on this. People did not possess a lot of clothes anyway, so a rope across the room easily sufficed. In my first year at secondary school in 1971, I was given a small, second-hand wooden suitcase. It was very small but I was so happy that, for the first time, in my life, I had a personal space where I could put my few clothes and other personal items. I could now take care of my own clothes, away from others' gaze - and from insects. I was very proud of that suitcase, it made me feel quite grown up.

I finally got a brand new suitcase in 1974. It was bought for me by my cousin Idris in Mombasa, after I had completed my fourth year in secondary school. What's more, I was allowed to choose one for myself. I can still remember that the price was fifty-three Kenya Shillings, around four to five pounds at that time. This was a huge sum of money for me and I was a really happy girl.

Around the same time, John bought me some brand new clothes in a shop called "Deacons" in Mombasa. A lovely former classmate and friend of mine, Agnes, was a shop assistant there. Deacons was considered to be an expensive shop, the local equivalent of M&S. We bought a flared, green skirt and a pink blouse. Before this, I had always worn dresses, because they were cheaper than a skirt and blouse. I thought I looked very smart and I wore this outfit every other day when I was going to college. So there I was with new clothes from Deacons and a new suitcase. I felt I was now a young woman, no longer just a girl.

STORY-TIME

In the evening at home, after our supper, we would sit together and often told each other stories that we had read or made up. One evening I re-told my family a story that I had read in one of the *Kiswahili* books at school. It is typical of the kind of stories we told each other, so I will tell it again here. I have changed the characters' names to make them easier for you to remember. The story goes like this: Once upon a time, there lived a man called Rashid, who was poor but cunning. People in his village thought he was strange, particularly because he lived alone. One day, Rashid was bored and went in search of something to occupy himself. It was a lovely, sunny day so, taking his machete with him, he went out to look for firewood. After walking for a while, he saw one especially beautiful tree with shapely branches. He stopped beneath it and looked up, so as to choose which branch to cut. Having made his decision, he climbed up the tree and sat on the branch. As he was cutting the branch, a man he knew called Ali, saw him sitting on the branch and called up to him: "You are sitting badly on that branch and when the branch falls, you will also fall!" Rashid called back: "Oh no, I won't. I won't fall, this is the way I always sit when I'm cutting a branch. This isn't my first time to cut one, you know!" Annoyed at Rashid's harsh tone, Ali walked off. Rashid continued hacking at the branch and, sure enough, when the branch was cut right through, he fell down along with it. He stood up and brushed himself down. Luckily for him, he wasn't hurt when he fell, just grazed and bruised. He stood still for a while, thinking about Ali's prediction that he would fall. He picked up the branch and headed home, feeling rather sore.

The next day, Rashid decided to look for Ali and tell him that he had been right, that he had fallen down with the branch. He arrived at Ali's house and called, "Hodi! Hodi!"(Knock knock!). Ali politely replied, "*Karibu*", meaning, "You are welcome, come in".

Rashid went in, and said, "Yesterday when I was cutting that branch, you told me I was going to fall down. You were right, because I did fall down with the branch. I think you must be a psychic. So, please, could you tell me when I will die?"

"What!" Ali said in surprise.

"You told me yesterday that I was going to fall off the tree and indeed I did fall," Rashid said.

"I said you would fall because you were sitting badly on the branch and I could see what was going to happen. But that doesn't mean I can tell you when you're going to die," Ali said.

But Rashid continued to demand to know when he was going to die. Ali thought for a while, and then said, "The day you take your horse for a ride and it trips up three times before you reach your destination, that will be the day you die".

Some days later, Rashid decided to ride his horse to visit a friend in another village quite a distance away. He prepared his horse and gave it a good drink of water before setting out. After a while, Rashid felt that his horse was not going fast enough. He shouted at the horse and tapped it with his stick. The horse then began to go faster… and faster — and then it stumbled. Still, Rashid urged it on, and the horse stumbled a second time. Then Rashid remembered what Ali had said, and grew afraid. If his horse tripped a third time, he thought, that would be the end of his life. But he kept urging it to move faster. Just before Rashid arrived at his friend's village, the horse tripped for a third time. Thinking that he was about to die, Rashid stopped the horse and got off. He lay down on the ground, covered himself with his *kikoi* and remained there without moving, the horse standing patiently beside him. Thinking he must be dead, Rashid lay still on the ground for three days and nights, neither eating nor drinking.

On the third day, a man happened to pass by and saw Rashid lying on the ground covered with his *kikoi*. He asked Rashid for directions to a certain village. Rashid replied that he knew where the village was when he was alive, but now he was dead and resting he was sorry, but he couldn't help. Surprised, the man said, "But you are still alive! You're talking!" Rashid, however, insisted that he was a dead man, and he continued to lie motionless on the ground. The man left, shaking his head.

Sometime later, a group of men on horseback passed Rashid, still lying on the ground covered with a *kikoi*. One of the men called out. Rashid could hear them, but made no movement. In his mind, he was dead. Another man from the group nudged the body, to see if it responded. Rashid still did not move. Another of the men whacked him with a stick, just to be sure. This hurt, but Rashid lay still, certain he was dead. The men, too, believed he was dead, so they rode off.

By this time, the people in Rashid's village were becoming very concerned because he hadn't been seen for days, which was unusual. They decided to go and look for him. They walked in the direction in which he'd been seen setting off on his horse. Nearly all the villagers went to look for Rashid, and after walking for a few hours, they found him on the ground, still covered with his *kikoi*. They tried to wake him up but he remained lying there without moving.

One of the villagers had an idea. "Rashid!" he cried, "get up, the end of the world has come."

With a start, Rashid struggled to his feet. Surrounding him were the familiar faces of his neighbours. He got dressed and returned to the village with them. He gave his horse away, just in case it tripped up three times again —

Rashid didn't want to die again! One of his village friends asked him what it was like to be dead. Rashid responded that there was nothing in to look forward to in heaven.

"People here on earth always say there is a good life waiting for them in heaven. Well, it's not true. All I experienced there was people poking me and hitting me. There wasn't even anything to eat or drink there!"

Rashid told his neighbours that now he knew what heaven was like, he was happy to be alive, and indeed, he lived happily ever after — at least until he really did die!

A STORY FROM MATA

This next story was told me by one of my schoolmates, who lived in a village called Mata, about fifteen kilometres from Eldoro, and concerns a husband and wife. The man liked his alcohol; he started drinking from an early age, and every day after working hard in his farm, he got drunk. When he reached a certain age he decided he ought to get married, and, after finding the right woman and paying the dowry, that was what he did. After getting married, he continued to drink. He would tell his wife he was going out, and did not say where. Being a good African wife, she did not ask him where he was going — women do not question their husband. After some time, she became a bit concerned that her husband was always going out and she began to suspect that he had another woman "on the side." She was determined to find out what he was up to, so one evening after he got home, she rather nervously asked him if they could have a little chat. He agreed, and they went and sat down in the sitting room, which was more comfortable. Seated next to her husband, the woman noticed that he was smelling of alcohol.

Wife: Do you drink beer?
Man: Yes
Wife: How many beers a day?
Man: Usually about three.
Wife: How much do you pay for each beer?
Man: One hundred shillings, including a tip.
Wife: And how long have you been drinking?
Man: About twenty years.
Wife: So a beer costs one hundred shillings, and you drink three a day. That makes it nine thousand shillings every month. If I'm not mistaken, it will be about one hundred and eight thousand shillings a year.
Man: Correct.
Wife: If in one year you spend one hundred and eight thousand, then over twenty years you have spent over two million shillings!
Man: Correct.
Wife: Do you realise that if you had not drunk so much beer, that money could have been put into a savings account? And after adding the interest, you could have bought an aeroplane!
Man: Do you drink?
Woman: No!
Man: Then, where is your aeroplane?

RELIGIOUS BELIEF

Almost all Africans have some sort of religious belief. People who declare themselves to be atheists are frowned upon, and Africans can be very direct when they disapprove of you. To illustrate this, in 1979 I was working as a clerical officer in Kenyatta High School in Mwatate, Kenya. A man who worked in the same school came to our house — we lived on the school compound. I knew him well, so I invited him inside. I addressed him as "baba," which is a sign of respect and we sat down in the sitting room. We had a long chat, mostly about the school and its problems. Suddenly, he said, "Aisha, you are a lovely person, and I am sorry that you will go to Hell." I didn't quite know what to say to this. I asked him why he thought it was so. He said that I did not follow his religion, and the only way to Heaven was through his religion. Some African people, as I said, can be so direct. In our African society, it is disrespectful to argue with someone older than you, so all I said was, "Let God be the judge."

A similar thing happened when we lived in China. A Chinese friend of ours told me that John and I would go to Hell because we did not embrace her religion. John, she said, might accept Jesus on his last breath, and the door to Heaven would be opened to him. As for me, I didn't have a chance! There was no way I would ever get to Heaven. She told me she would pray for me and, with a bit of luck, I might get to Heaven through her prayers, but she couldn't guarantee it. I can only think she made this distinction because I was black. I am still in touch with her on social media, and I guess she still prays for me. I cannot accept how someone can be so direct and tell others that they would go to Hell! Why would someone go out of their way to say that to anyone? It can be upsetting to be told that you're going to Hell. You don't need a diploma to know that what you say can sometimes hurt others. She should have been more considerate of my feelings. Nowadays, however, I don't get upset, I just feel sorry for such people.

Life in Africa can be hard, and I think it helps people to believe in a life after death. As far as I am concerned, what you believe doesn't matter, as long as it does not harm or upset anyone. Only by being tolerant of diversity can we all live happily together despite our differences. I have very much enjoyed and welcomed the diversity I have encountered in my life and have found it is good to learn from others.

MAPS — WHO NEEDS THEM!

A lot of African people don't know how to read a map, and I am one of them. People in the rural areas of my youth had no need of maps, because they mostly walked familiar paths or used public transport; you get on a bus that takes you where you want to go, then get off when you arrive. The route you took hardly matters to you. If someone is going to visit a friend or family member, they will be told how to get there and which bus to get, and the person they are visiting meets them at the other end. If the person travelling is not quite sure where to get off, the bus driver or other passengers will tell them. Nowadays many people have mobile phones, and can communicate with the person they are visiting — and journeys are mostly made in order to visit someone. I am told that over half of the people in the world now use a smartphone that will tell them exactly where to go when they are making a journey, so they won't need to use maps either. They are becoming just like us Africans!

Donating blood

People in England often donate blood, whereas in Kenya and Tanzania people will tend only donate blood to members of their family, or come from the same ethic group. If blood is donated to a stranger or blood bank, payment may be demanded. It's a shame. When I was working at Kenyatta High School, a request was made to the school for blood donations for someone who had been admitted to a nearby hospital and urgently needed a transfusion. The first thing people asked was, "What tribe are they?"

Firewood

A lot of villagers in Kenya and Tanzania still use firewood for cooking. When I was growing up there was no other source of fuel. In fact we did not know that there might be an alternative, except perhaps for charcoal. Charcoal was sold, but not everyone could afford it, and firewood was free! People in big towns and cities were forced to resort to charcoal or gas. Even now, my family living in rural villages of Tanzania and Kenya are still using firewood.

Even in this Derbyshire village many of us use wood fires to keep us warm.

The firewood we use in Kenya and Tanzania consists mainly of branches fallen from the trees. Sometimes people use big logs, but these have to be split with an axe. I was allowed by my family to use an axe when I was only about twelve years old. When we were in England, John wanted to buy a hand-axe for chopping wood, and he had to prove that he was over eighteen before anyone would sell him one! The only problem with using firewood for cooking is that the pot gets very black on the outside, and it is difficult to clean. The *sufuria* (pot) is left unwashed on the outside, and accumulates a thick layer of soot.

When I was growing up, fire played a very big part in our lives. We used fire for comfort, cooking meals, making tea, heating water, keeping us warm. We gathered near the fire to talk and exchange news. We did not have electricity, so we relied on wood fires for all sorts of things. Sometimes we used fire as a torch if we had to go outside at night. Luckily, my family now has electricity, which has made a big difference to their lives; yet they still use firewood for cooking. In the villages, the kitchen is usually a separate building from the main house, because of the smoke from the wood fire. When we are cooking, the door and the windows are opened to allow the smoke, or as much as possible, to escape. Even now my family will leave their kitchen door and windows open until quite late in the evening to allow the smoke to dissipate. When the door is left open, however, mosquitoes get in and hide in the dark corners. To discourage mosquitoes, people sometimes put dried cow dung or wild lavender in a small container with hot charcoal and the smoke drives most of the mosquitoes away. I did not use the cow dung to chase away mosquitoes, I preferred the smell of lavender!

Our children and grandchildren did not have the experience of using firewood to cook and they would not even know how to do so. They have been lucky in many ways not to have to have lived the sort of life I led when I was much younger. There were many things that I enjoyed then and miss, but life was also very challenging at times. For me they were experiences that I learned from, and gave me a basis on which to reflect and compare with life in England and other countries. Sometimes I feel I have lived two separate lives, the cultures are so different, but I feel that who I am now is a mixture of cultures which I have chosen for myself.

COOKING POTS

Sufurias are large aluminium pots with wide rims but no handle. People also used clay pots. My mother preferred these, and even made her own pots, which she also used to sell in the local markets. Occasionally, she would use a *sufuria* for rice, *sima* (maize meal), tea or porridge because they are better suited to being cooked in a *sufuria* than a clay pot. Clay pots can leave bits of grit in the food, especially if you mash it up with a spoon. Clay pots are therefore better for cooking foods that don't need much stirring, like sweet potatoes, stew, cassava, kidney beans and green bananas.

We did not possess oven gloves, and none of the pots had a handle, so we used bits of cloth torn from old clothes to pick them up. Sometimes we used to risk using our bare hands. To this day, John tells me I must have asbestos hands when he sees me picking up a hot plate or baking tray without using oven gloves.

All of the cooking is done on a wood fire which needs constant refuelling with branches from the wood pile. So that this can be done easily, the *sufurias* or clay pots are placed on three stones arranged in a triangle and the firewood fed through the gaps between the stones. For my aunt Khadija this fireplace had an extra use. She used to keep her cash in a glass bottle, which she placed in a hole she had dug beside one of the cooking stones as a secure hiding place, covering the hole with soil and ash and levelling it so no one could see it. That was her bank!

People in rural areas tended not to keep their money in a bank but put their cash under their mattress or in a tin kept under the bed. Since mobile phones have become widely available, most money transfers between accounts are now carried out using mobile phones. There is a banking app called *Mpesa* that is very popular, but for everyday shopping, cash is still widely used, as far as I am aware. In the past, going to the bank was a tedious and costly process. For example, teachers in rural schools had to travel long distances to the nearest bank in order to collect their pay. Since all teachers got paid on the same day, at the end of each month there were long queues at the bank. This, combined with the bank's demand for all sorts of forms to be filled in for any transaction, meant that it often took more than half a day to withdraw any money.

PRESERVING FOOD

The villages of Kitoghoto and Eldoro didn't have electricity, which meant they had no fridges. For much of what we ate, this didn't really matter because we had fresh food available from our farms for most of the time. The difficulty arose when it came to meat. Most people kept livestock — goats, cows and chickens — for food. Occasionally they might buy meat from the butcher in Taveta town. If they wanted more than a kilo or two, however - for special occasions such as a wedding, or Idd-il-Fitr (the feast of the end of Ramadhan), or when there was a special visitor – they would slaughter an animal. It was quite common to slaughter a chicken which would easily be eaten up by a family in a day. If a goat or a cow was slaughtered, however, not all the meat would be consumed at once, so the remainder would be salted to preserve it. This was done by first cutting the meat into long strips and then rubbing it thoroughly with roughly ground salt in a *sufuria*. The salted strips were then hung from the ceiling above the fire for a few days to dry them, before storing them in a column of stacked *sufurias*. These fitted tightly on top of each other so that there were no gaps for flies or other insects to get to the meat. They were kept in the kitchen, where it is always dry.

In the villages where I grew up, it was the custom for whoever had slaughtered a cow to give some of the meat to neighbours. This meat was put on to sharpened wooden skewers – like giant kebabs - before being shared out. This sharing was our way of bonding with our neighbours, a sign of mutual dependence that was important for us in many situations: a bicycle to transport a patient to hospital, someone to look after a child for a few hours, and so on. I find the same sense of mutual support in the village I now live in, in England. Without 'spying' or intruding, we keep an eye on vulnerable neighbours. When we are snowed up in winter – as we are as I am writing this - a neighbour with snow-proof transport might offer to do shopping for us. It is these small things that build a sense of community amongst us. Is this a 'village thing'? My experience of living in, say, Mombasa, suggests to me that it is.

Later, when we lived in a Chinese city, I was fascinated to see that people preserved food in a similar way to us. They would, for example, dry fish, meat, homemade sausages and sliced young bamboo shoots by laying them out on a mat or sheet of plastic and putting them out in the sun. This was common practice even in the large, modern city where we lived. It was quite normal to see food laid out to dry on the pavements, by the side of the road, on the riverbanks, wherever there was a free space. I asked one of my Chinese friends why they dried their sausages and fish in the street, because to me drying the meat or fish in the open street with dust in the air, people walking and some spitting, and cars driven by was rather unhygienic. Her response was that the food would be cooked before being eaten, killing off any germs, so there was no need to worry!

EATING MEAT

In my village, the slaughtering of a cow or a goat was a man's job. Very rarely, a woman might slaughter a chicken, which I guess is an easier job. I was brought up as a

Muslim, instructed only to eat meat from an animal that has been killed by another Muslim in the correct way. The animal's throat must be cut so that it bleeds to death. Meat killed this way is called "Halal" meat. Muslims will not eat meat slaughtered by a non-Muslim. Some very strict Muslims will not eat any food at all that has been prepared by a non-Muslim, because they fear that their cooking pans might have been used previously to cook pork, which Muslims are forbidden to eat.

When I was living in Eldoro, we were friends with a *Kamba* lady, a devoted Catholic, whose first language was *Kikamba*, so we communicated in *Kiswahili*. Once, we took her a gift of some food. She welcomed us into her house and offered us something to eat, but our family had told us never to eat any food cooked by a non-Muslim. We were embarrassed, because we really liked this lady and wanted to accept. Not wishing to be rude, we told her we had just had lunch, and were full ("*tumeshiba*"), but we thanked her for the offer. Later, my family seemed to have become less strict about these rules, and we were told it was all right to eat her food, as long as it wasn't meat. I was pleased, because the *Kamba* lady used to make very nice boboro — a mixture of maize seeds and kidney beans — that was much tastier than the boboro we had at home.

Eventually, the lady and her family moved back to their home town, north of Nairobi and hundreds of miles from our village. We missed them very much, but in those days, the only means of communication was by letter, and this lady hadn't been to school, so she could neither read nor write. Telephones were not available to us or her. In fact, the first time I ever used a telephone was in 1975, when I was living in Mombasa. I did not even know which way up the receiver went — which was the speaking end and which the listening end!

Toothbrushing

When I was growing up, we didn't have toothbrushes as you might know them. We used twigs from trees to clean our teeth. We would break off a twig and peel the bark off just at one end, chewing the stick at that end until it became frayed, like a brush – a toothbrush! Neither did we use toothpaste. People in the village were not familiar with any other kind of tooth brush, nor toothpaste of any kind. We knew of no other way of cleaning our teeth except the one I have described, and we assumed that everyone cleaned their teeth the same way as us. The first time I saw plastic toothbrushes was in 1969 in a shop in Taveta town. In our village, Eldoro, there was only one, small shop, which sold the basics, such as loose tea, sugar, salt, maize meal and other small items, but certainly no toothbrushes. In any case, a "proper" toothbrush cost money! People preferred to spend what cash they had on essentials, like tea, sugar and salt. Why waste money when we had toothbrushes that were just as good, and moreover were free!

Not all trees are a good source of toothbrushes, because some are too hard. We brushed our teeth once a day — before breakfast, which you might find strange. No one brushed their teeth before they went to bed and we knew that members of neighbouring families followed the same routine. Having no sink or running water in the house, we all brushed our teeth outside, and that is how we knew! Despite only cleaning them once a day - and before eating too - our teeth were generally very good, probably because of our diet, which had very little sugar in it. In Kenya sweets were a rare treat for special occasions. When I was a child, someone in the family might visit a nearby town and bring me and my sister one sweet each, although this did not happen often. We would each suck our sweet very slowly to make it last. I only started brushing my teeth twice a day when I came to England in 1984, but I am fortunate not to have a sweet tooth, even to this day.

Even when I visited Kenya and Tanzania in 2022, my relatives still only brushed their teeth in the mornings before breakfast, just as I had done when I was a child. We brushed our teeth to freshen up our mouth after sleeping and before breakfast, rather than as a way to keep our teeth healthy. The only thing that has changed about teeth cleaning in my family in Africa is that they no longer use chewed twigs but plastic toothbrushes and toothpaste. For them, this is seen as a social upgrade and now they can afford to buy such things.

My father died at eighty-five with all his teeth intact. His brother, Mbaraka, who is eighty-four, still has a full set of even, white teeth. A friend recently sent me a video of her daughter's birthday party with other children. The children were very happily singing and dancing and on the table near them were lots of cakes, a plateful of sweets and bottles of sugary drinks. It was lovely to see them so happy but I found myself hoping they brush their teeth twice a day!

FALSE TEETH

When I was living in Usangi, some of the villagers — my mother being one — had lost teeth for one reason or another. An example was my mother. The village "madman" had hit her in the face, knocking out one of her teeth. We had never heard of dentures or replacement teeth and she lived with her gap until she died. In the early nineteen fifties no one ever thought of replacing a missing tooth.

I first saw someone with dentures in 1979 when my English parents-in-law came to visit us in Kenya. "Wow! What lovely smiles they have," I thought, their teeth were so white and even. The following morning I went into the bathroom and saw jars with teeth floating in them! "How did this happen?" I wondered. How did these floating teeth get to the bathroom? If our children had seen them, they would probably have been scared. I discovered that the dentures belonged to our visitors and that people do not sleep wearing their dentures, but it was many years later that I learnt this from my patients in the hospital where I worked.

When I worked for the NHS, one of my duties was cleaning the patients' dentures. At first I found it quite repellent. I felt sorry for the patients, who must have felt uncomfortable about it, as it's a rather personal thing. Some people might think I am making a big fuss about this, but do remember that I had never had any previous experience of people wearing 'false teeth'. Well, almost never.

The mentally disturbed

Remembering my mother's unfortunate encounter with the village "madman" brings to mind the way villagers treated the mentally ill. Family members with mental problems were generally cared for, but this sometimes proved difficult, especially if they tended to wander off. With so many other responsibilities, it could be hard to watch them all the time, and most families could not afford to employ a helper. Some people were left to wander, as long as they stayed within the village; sometimes they could be trusted to return home by themselves, depending on the severity of their mental problems.

There were two boys in the village of Usangi who used to go round pulling the flowers from people's graves. Knowing the boys were ill, the villagers took their behaviour in good part. If they wandered too far from home, someone from the family would go and look for them and bring them back. This was the general case in villages that I knew of. No one harmed or abused them. People in Usangi would say that a person who ill-treats someone with mental problems will have children with similar problems. They might say, "*utapata dhambi kwa Mungu*," meaning 'You will be a sinner in the eyes of God.' As most people in the villages are religious, they took this saying seriously.

When I was a child, there were no shelters, no psychiatric care. As far as I know, this is still the case today — at least in rural areas. People with disabilities in the cities or towns may be treated a lot worse than those in the rural villages. People call them names, and they are less likely to be cared for; many are abandoned. In the rural areas families which have money may employ someone to take care of their relatives in need. For example, when my aunt Khadija, who brought me up, was getting old she needed help moving around, as well as with washing and dressing, so I employed my half-sister to take care of her.

WOMEN'S WORK

When I was living in the villages, women spent most of their time working on the land. If they had spare time they might weave baskets and mats from palm leaves. Some men also made baskets, but not mats for some reason. Most of the baskets and mats were made to be used in the home, but some were sold in the market so as to get a bit of extra cash. My aunt Khadija and her husband made baskets which she then sold and they used the money they made to buy sugar, paraffin and clothes. They did not need to buy food, because they grew their own in their relatively large farm, where they planted staples such as maize, cassava, sweet potatoes, yams and rice, and also vegetables — okra, cabbage, spinach, kidney beans, mung beans. They had fruit trees too — pawpaws, mangoes, lemons, limes, bananas and tomatoes. My favourite was tamarind. I have never seen tamarind on sale in England, so I was delighted to find it in Dubai when we were visiting our daughter who lives there.

I was pretty good at climbing trees to pick fruit. The only fruit trees I hesitated to climb were mangoes and tamarinds; not that they were hard to climb, but they had very thick foliage and the branches were close together, making them very dark but also dangerous for climbers. Snakes like to hide in them. On the one occasion I did decide to climb a tamarind tree, and I found a snake waiting for me! The snake, being green itself was particularly hard to see among the leaves. I climbed down that tree in record time! The best way to get the fruits down safely from tamarind and mango trees is to use a long pole. Most of us could not – and did not try to - differentiate between venomous and non-venomous snakes. If you try to look closely enough to tell the difference, they can bite or spit at you, and then it is too late. Some of the most deadly snakes are found in trees, and don't always escape when disturbed. So snakes are always killed on sight, it's not worth taking the risk!

Bees

African bees can be very dangerous. When John and I were living in Mwatate, we one day found a swarm of bees hanging on a tree just outside our house. We were particularly worried for our children, since a child who is stung many times - for instance, if attacked by a swarm - can die. We did not know how to handle this situation. In England, you can just call on a pest removal company; not so in rural Mwatate. One of our neighbours suggested we light a fire beneath the tree, so that the smoke would drive the bees away. So, we duly set a fire going, but the bees did not budge. Now they were buzzing even more menacingly, shooting in and out of the tree; they were obviously protecting the queen. Next, we tried hacking off the branch the bees were hanging from, which was a rather dangerous thing to do. We hit the branch a couple of times, then raced indoors before they could attack us. We repeated the procedure until the branch — and the bees — fell to the ground. Now we had a swarm on the ground to deal with. In the end, we decided to "fire-bomb" the swarm. We took a bottle of kerosene and stuffed a cloth into the neck, which we lit: a real Molotov cocktail! We threw this at the bees, and ran. We watched in horrified fascination as the kamikaze bees flew in and out of the burning swarm, doing their utmost to protect the queen. We were sorry to have to do this, but it was either the bees or our children!

HONEY

Considering what I have just said about the dangers of African bees, you might be surprised to know that people do in fact collect honey from the hives of wild bees — and enjoy eating it! They do it like this: First, the men — never the women, as far as I know — hang hollowed-out logs in trees near the village; but not too close to the houses. With luck, a swarm will pick one or more of these to build a hive in. The men wait, watching the hive until they are sure there is honey in it. Before collecting the honey, usually working in pairs, they cover themselves in cloth or sheets of plastic to protect themselves from the stings. Underneath the tree, they light a fire of damp wood so that it is smoky. This drives most of the bees out of the hive, although they don't go far, and they keep trying to get back in. One of the two men will keep the fire smoking, while his companion climbs up to the hive and reaches in, covered in furious bees, and snatches as many honeycombs as he can. He leaves one or two combs so that the bees will make more honey. As you can imagine, it is hard, even dangerous, work, but is worth it for the delicious honey!

The honey wasn't separated from the comb. We chewed the whole thing, swallowing the honey and spitting out the waxy remains. The taste of Kenyan honey is different from that of English honey, since the flowers from which the bees take the nectar are different. Personally, I prefer the wild honey I ate as a child. When I came to England, I was surprised to see English people using honey and lemon in hot water as a remedy for coughs or colds; in Kenya, such a drink is thought to be very dangerous. When we were living in Mwatate, John developed a cough, and suggested that a drink of hot water with honey and lemon would soothe his throat. I was horrified. I told him it would make him ill. Naturally, he didn't believe me, since he had often been given it as a child, he said. But when he tried it in Mwatate, the result was a terrible stomach ache. John was puzzled, so we tried a little experiment. We put a bit of honey in a saucer and squeezed lemon juice onto it. The honey started sizzling and bubbling. Evidently, the honey in Kenya has different properties from that in England.

A CHILDREN'S STORY

When I was in Primary School, our *Kiswahili* teacher sometimes used to read us stories from a book called *Hekaya za Abunuwas na Hadithi Nyingine* ("The legend of Abunuwas and other stories"). This was a collection of traditional tales passed down from generation to generation, some of which are short and very funny.

One of the stories goes like this: Once upon a time, there lived a very poor old man called Edward (I have changed the names of the characters for English readers), and his wife, Winnie. They had one son, whom they called Robert. One day, a rich man called Zakaria visited the family and, seeing how poor they were, he suggested to Robert that if he spent one whole night standing in the sea on his own, he, Zakaria, would give him twenty dinari. Now, twenty dinari was a huge sum of money for Robert and his family, so he accepted the offer. Winnie was very anxious at the thought of her son spending a whole night on his own in the cold, cold sea. So she decided she would sit outside their house all night, shining a torch towards the sea so she could keep an eye on her boy and be sure he was safe. On the appointed night, Robert went out into the sea. But Zakaria saw the light from the torch, so, when Robert went for his twenty dinari, Zakaria refused to pay. "Your mother made a fire to keep you warm. You weren't in the sea at all, you were just next to it in the warmth of the fire!" Robert explained that there was no fire by the sea, it was just his mother shining a torch at him because she was worried for his safety, like any mother. But Zakaria would have none of it. He insisted that Robert was lying. So, Robert decided to take Zakaria to court to get him to hand over the money he had been promised. To support him with his case, Robert went to see Abunuwasi, a man well-known for his knowledge of the law. Even more than that, however, Abunuwasi was known for his cunning.

Robert described what Zakaria had done. Abunuwasi

said he was willing to help but on one condition, that he would get a share of Robert's money. Robert asked Abunuwasi how much he would charge. Abunuwasi replied that he would like fifteen dinari. Robert was outraged. "Come on! That would leave me with only five dinari. That's not fair!" "Okay," Abunuwasi said, "Then let's each have half." Robert had no choice. At least, he thought, ten was still quite a bit of money, so he agreed to give Abunuwasi half the money. Abunuwasi then advised Robert to go to the Sultan and tell him the whole story. Robert took his advice, and nervously approached the Sultan and presented his case. Unfortunately, the Sultan agreed with Zakaria that the light from the torch was strong enough to give Robert some warmth, when he was supposed to be in the dark and cold all on his own. Besides being a rich man, Zakaria was one of his best friends and he did not want to upset him. Robert was very disappointed but not surprised because, poor as he was, he did not really expect the Sultan to support him. He went back to Abunuwasi and told him that the Sultan had refused to help. Abunuwasi said to Robert, "I know that, through the will of God, you will get your money tomorrow."

The next day, Abunuwasi decided to hold a party for everyone in the village, including the Sultan and Zakaria. He went to the local market and bought a live goat, rice, cooking oil, curry powder and other spices ready for the party. The goat was slaughtered, the meat cut into pieces and put into one of his cooking pots, while the rice was put into another. He then made the fire and went back to his guests. The guests — including the Sultan and Zakaria —

were directed to sit and wait in Abunuwasi's living room. They all knew one another, so they chatted happily together while they waited for the expected food and drinks. They waited and waited, but no food and drink came, even though they had been invited for lunch and it was getting rather late. The guests began to grow very hungry and restless, and eventually, the Sultan dashed into the kitchen to find out why the food was taking such a long time. To his astonishment, the fire was certainly lit but the rice and the meat were sitting some distance from the flames, still only slightly warmed.

The Sultan was very angry. He said to Abunuwasi, "We have all been here since before midday and the sun is almost setting, but still we have not been offered any food! I am going to tell everyone to go home." Abunuwasi said politely, "Please, Sultan, don't be angry, the food will be ready soon." The Sultan pointed at the pans and said, "That food will never be ready, never in ten years."

Abunuwasi said, "Do you remember when Robert came to get your advice about your friend Zakaria's refusal to pay him after he'd spent one whole night in the cold sea?" The Sultan nodded. "The reason your friend Zakaria gave for not paying Robert was that he thought Robert was warming himself in the warmth from his mother's torch. That being the case, I am also warming the rice and the goat meat in the same way." He went on, "Remember, Robert's mother, Winnie, only used the torch to keep an eye on her son from her house, because like any loving parent, she was worried. How could her son feel the warmth from the torch from such a long distance away?" Abunuwasi told the Sultan that Robert deserved to be paid all of his money. Feeling ashamed, the Sultan asked no more questions, and ordered his friend Zakaria to pay Robert all the money he'd been promised. He duly paid Robert the full amount. Moreover, kind Abunuwasi declined his share.

After Robert had been paid, Abunuwasi ordered the food to be cooked properly, and so, even though they had missed lunch, they enjoyed their supper, and everyone ate their fill. They were entertained with traditional drums, music and dancing too. A happy ending for everyone.

TREES

I don't remember people planting trees in the villages where I lived, although there were plenty around. Maybe they were self-seeded. However, when I was at Eldoro Primary School, the teachers organised tree-planting days for us. There were trees around the school which gave welcome shade as well as improving the appearance of the school, but there were many gaps and the idea was to fill these gaps with new trees. We pupils also made use of the trees to hang up our lunches that brought from home. We did not know the names of most of the trees around us. The exceptions were the many different kinds of fruit trees that grew locally. If we planted fruit trees around the school, however, we thought they would tempt passers-by to pick the fruits, which we did not want to encourage. If anyone was going to pick fruits from the trees we had planted it should be us!

More seriously though, fruit trees would also attract baboons who steal fruits from trees in the farms. They were already often stealing our lunches hanging in the trees and damaging the trees. If you are not used to baboons and perhaps think they look funny, even cute, I must point out that they can in fact be very violent towards young children in particular – not animals that you want hanging around a primary school.

One tree whose name we did know was the acacia, but this is another one that we never planted near the school. They bear long, thin, sharp thorns that litter the ground beneath most acacias. The primary school children from the village would mostly either be barefoot or wear thin sandals. If you ever happened to have the misfortune to tread on an acacia thorn, you would certainly remember it for a long time. Acacia trees and primary schools don't go together!

Sadly, Kenya is becoming increasingly deforested. People cut trees for all sorts of purposes — building houses, making charcoal and simply for firewood for cooking or heating the home. People who have little or no education often do not realise the importance of trees. As a result, some of the landscapes in Kenya that I knew as a child are now bare and barren because of people cutting too many trees. In contrast, Tanzania does seem to undertake many tree-planting programmes. At least, it always appears to me to be much greener than Kenya.

ANOTHER ONE OF MY FAVOURITE STORIES

As I said before, we did not have time to read books at home because we were so busy. But I managed somehow to squeeze in some time for reading, especially stories written in *Kiswahili* and which were short enough for me to complete in the little time available. This story is one of my favourites.

Once upon a time there lived a man called Jay. Jay was very cunning. He lived with his wife in a village called Kirongaya, close to the sea. Jay's fellow villagers disliked him because he was dishonest. He was a poor man and had little to live on, so he tricked people to get what he wanted from them, and being pretty bright, he got away with it. The village chief was comfortably-off but in the village there was also a much richer man called David, who was respected because of how kind he was. The villagers grew more and more fed up with Jay and his cunning tricks until eventually they had had enough of him. David then suggested to them that the only way to punish Jay was by throwing him into a big hole in the ground which they knew had a solitary lion living in it, and Jay would be eaten alive. So, the people of the village tied Jay to a rope and lowered him into the hole. They had expected Jay to scream and struggle, but he was strangely calm. Jay, you see, had a plan. His plan was to make a friend of the lion. The villagers duly lowered Jay into the hole, and he at once started stroking the lion, talking to it as if they had known each other for years. The people from the village went off, pleased finally to be rid of Jay. Now, over the years, the villagers had got into the habit of occasionally dropping fresh meat into the hole for the lion. When they next did so, Jay caught the meat as it fell, and shared it with the lion. After Jay had been in the hole for four days, a man from the village happened to be passing by the hole when he heard a voice coming from inside it.

He wondered whose voice it could be, since he was convinced Jay must be dead. He stepped closer to the hole, being careful not to disturb the lion. The closer he got, the louder the voice became, until he recognised the voice as Jay's. He leaned over the edge and peered in. He could not believe his eyes when he saw Jay talking to the lion and stroking it. The man ran back to the village and told everyone what he had seen, including the rich man, David. The other villagers all thought he was talking nonsense; there was no way Jay could still be alive. They carried on with their lives, and forgot all about Jay, who had never been popular anyway.

One day, another man from the same village was on his way to the beach. He walked slowly along the shore, admiring the deep blue sea, when, suddenly, he spotted a human arm sticking up out of the water, with three fingers sticking up. He asked himself, "*Huo mkono ni* wa *jini*?" (Is that a devil's arm?) The man ran back to the village and told the others, including the chief, what he had seen. They were all puzzled. The chief and his followers went to take a look at this arm with three fingers sticking out of the sea. Nervously, they waded into the water to try and pull out the arm. But every time they got close, the arm would disappear. They were astonished and did not know what to do next. Then someone suggested that if Jay had still been alive, he would probably have been able to explain this strange phenomenon. The chief ordered two men to go to the hole and see if Jay really was dead as they'd assumed up until then. As they approached the hole, the two men shouted out, "Jay, are you still alive?" To their great surprise, Jay called back loudly and clearly that he was indeed alive. The two men told him that the chief wanted to ask a favour of him. They asked him if he would agree to come out if they threw down a rope for him. Jay replied that he would like to come out to see his beloved wife and the chief, but he did not have any clothes to wear. The men said that was not a problem, they'd get him a *shuka*, a cloth that men wear wrapped around their waist. They threw down the *shuka*, but instead of tying it around his waist, he wrapped it around his head! The men called down again, asking him if he was now ready to come out. Jay told them that he was still naked. The men said, " But we have just thrown you a *shuka*!" Jay insisted that he needed more clothes, and he listed the items he required. The men brought him all the clothes he had asked for. So, Jay got dressed and said goodbye to the lion, stroking him gently. The two men lowered the rope and pulled him out.

The men took Jay to see the chief, who told him about the arm sticking out from the sea with three fingers raised upwards. The chief asked Jay what the meaning of what they had seen could be. Jay replied that he must go and see it for himself. But he asked if he could first have something to eat, because he had been eating raw meat since he had been put in the hole, and he was craving vegetables. After Jay had eaten, the chief and a group of people accompanied him to the seashore, where the arm with three fingers sticking up was still visible. He closed his eyes and mumbled a few words to himself. He raised his right hand with three fingers pointing up to the sky, just like the arm in the sea. Suddenly, one finger disappeared, leaving only two fingers sticking out! Jay continued to mumble and suddenly another finger disappeared, leaving just one finger raised. He mumbled on, and the last finger disappeared, together with the arm. All the people watching were amazed. How had Jay managed to make the arm and the three fingers disappear?

Jay explained to them that three fingers sticking out meant that there is no secret that can be shared among three people and remain a secret. The same applies when there are just two people — the secret will not be kept. Just one finger sticking out means a secret can only be kept when just one person keeps it to himself. The arm had disappeared once it knew that Jay had understood its message. The chief and his followers were delighted, and full of praise for Jay. As a reward, the chief gave Jay and his wife a lot of presents and a big house, where Jay and his wife lived happily for many years and eventually became popular with all the villagers.

My mum and I walking up to her home at Kirongaya
in the Pare Mountains, in 1988.

My father at his home in Chankuku in the Pare Mountains,
in the same year, with my son Mani (sitting) and my half-brother, Walii.

My aunt Khadija brought me up from the age of five. She was born in 1911 when East Africa was so different from when I grew up.
She taught me so much about our Pare customs and traditions and I will always be grateful for making me the Pare person I am today.

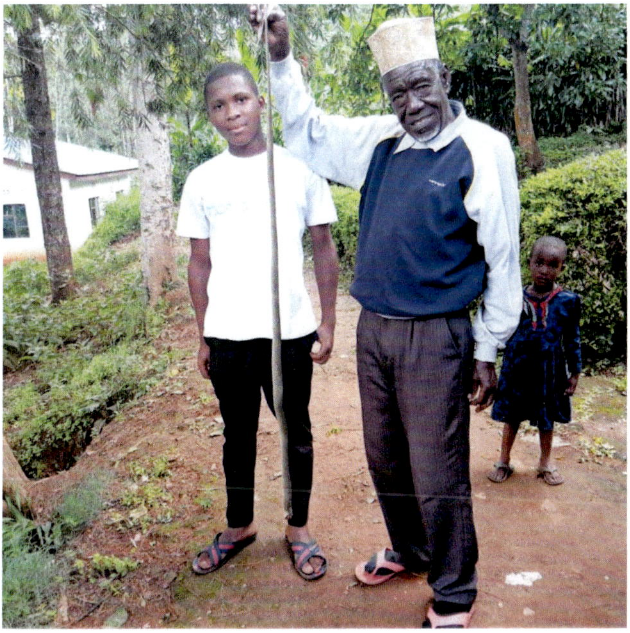

My uncle, Mbaraka, has just killed a snake that was entering his house in the Pare village of Chankuku. Two of his grandchildren look on.

Our children visit their African grandmother, my sister and various cousins (and a puppy) in Kisangara village, near the Pare Mountains.
We were on our roundabout way from the Solomon Islands to the UK.

Our daughter Tuni and our son-in-law Simon with their children, Savannah and Zain, on holiday in Spain in 2024 – to get some sunshine!

Getting the family hair all tangled together in Dubai are our daughter, Farida, our son-in-law, Jeremy, together with their children, Layla, Ezra and Sahara.

There's plenty of sunshine in 2025 for our son, Mani, granddaughter Aaliyah (with her precious cat, Milo), daughter-in-law, Umi, and our latest grandson, Damien, who is not quite sure what is going on; at their home in Redditch.

Our son Nurudin with his partner Gemma and their daughter Leah outside their home in 2024. Hasn't he grown since he was cuddling a puppy in the Kisangara picture!

This is Mr. Bakari outside his home in Eldoro village. I grew up within his family and he very kindly paid my school fees. This kindness, made all the difference to my future life options.

Mr. Bakari's wife Amina also brought me up and I learnt a lot from her, including how to grow outstanding crops of maize like the one she is rightly proud of in this picture.

My mum holding Mani's hand, me carrying Farida and my half-sister Mwanasha; outside our house in Mwatate.

John with my other half-sister, Zukira, in 1988, standing outside her home in Same, on the plains below the Pare Mountains, Tanzania.

What a contrast there is between the lush, green landscape of the Pare mountains (above) and the arid landscape of the plains surrounding them, where even the goats seek the shade (below). Notice the baobab tree in the background of the plains picture.

On whichever side of the Kenya/Tanzania border I was living, the beautiful Mount Kilimanjaro was always a companion. Above is a view from just outside Moshi, in Tanzania. Right is a picture taken from my school in Kenya – Eldoro High School. The building is the girls' dormitory; the tree is a papaya.

The communal water tap in Eldoro village: a place to get water for the home, exchange news and gossip and, in my case, get a few clothes washed. The Pare Mountains make a great backdrop whatever you are doing.

It's all a matter of balance and posture! Tuni and two cousins carry their loads the African way, having come down from the misty Pare mountains to catch a bus to Kenya.

The red soil gives away the location (and the age of this slide);
a netball match at Eldoro High School. I am in there somewhere.

Also at Eldoro High School, my experience of sitting on a motorbike, and certainly not part of regular school activities. The smile shows I enjoyed it, which was good thing because later in my life John had a motorbike and I rode with him.

Maize was our staple food in the village. You see me here pounding maize to de-husk it before cooking it in a pot on the fire, shown below. Roasted maize cobs were something else we really enjoyed while waiting for the maize in the pot to cook.

Mombasa where I studied at college to prepare for the world of work.

Age 21 and wondering what the future might hold for me.

Derbyshire, where I now live having experienced
and finally retired from the world of work.

At home in Derbyshire in 2021: John and I with our children and
grandchildren and most of their English cousins, aunts and uncles.

Chapter 2

Widening Horizons

Meeting cultural challenges: African and English

At the age of twenty-seven, I left East Africa behind and travelled to England with my husband and our four children. Even then, I knew somehow that I would never live in East Africa again. I was leaving my life and all the familiar ways behind. When the aeroplane touched down at Heathrow Airport just four days before Christmas, I had no idea what I would find, nor did the children, of course. Only John had experience of the cold, dark country we had arrived in, but even he, after having lived for twelve years in Kenya, suffered from culture shock. It was all new and exciting for me and the children, but it soon became clear that the England John remembered no longer existed. As he has since said, he thought he knew what to expect, but much took him by surprise.

The first thing we had to learn was to dress warmly. Every time we left the house, we had to put on multiple layers of clothing, big boots and woolly hats. It snowed the day after we arrived. The children were fascinated by the strange, beautiful sight of falling white flakes. Mani rushed outside to touch the snow and quickly learned that it is very, very cold; he had dashed out in bare feet! It was a time of very rapid learning and adjustment for the children. Mani and the others quickly realised that there would be many ways in which they were going to have to adapt to their new life and its culture. It was harder for me, I think. As an adult I was more set in my ways, and many of those ways turned out to be very different. I would have to make changes that often contradicted what I had always been taught. I had learned the "right" way to behave, and now the people I was living amongst expected me to behave otherwise. In my daily life, I was continually coming up against these contrasts, and in this chapter, I describe some of them.

Being a woman and being a man

When I went to live in England, I became very impressed by the way men helped around the house — cooking, cleaning, washing dishes and changing nappies. In most African countries, each of these is considered to be a woman's job. I had never seen a man changing a baby's nappy, for instance.

I remember seeing a man in our village sitting on a chair and watching his child crawling towards him. The child badly needed its nappy changing, but instead of doing it himself, even though he had nothing else to do, the man called his wife, who was already busy in the kitchen, to come and change it. Far from being annoyed, the wife accepted it as her job. Besides, women are taught not to question their husbands. African women are brought up to consider themselves inferior to men. They are taught this not only by men, but also by the older women in the family. While on the subject of nappies, I might add that in those days there were no disposable nappies, people used nappies made of cloth, which were washed and reused. Our first three children wore cloth nappies.

WALKING

I was impressed to see many English people going out walking for exercise and pleasure. In Kenya and Tanzania, people only walk when there is no other form of transport available. When John and I lived in Kenya, John used to encourage me to go for walks with him, so I was not entirely surprised at what I saw in England, but it was a comfort to learn that John was not as weird as I thought! People who saw us walking in Kenya would ask, "Haven't you got any work to do?" We would reply that, yes, we do have other work, but we had decided to go out for some fresh air and to admire the scenery. People would shake their heads as if to say we were obviously mad! It is not part of African culture for people to go for a walk just for fun. They might go to visit their friends or neighbours for a chat or to gossip, but not just walk for the sake of getting some exercise. I wonder if the reason for this is that people do a lot of physical work on the farms. This is especially the case with women, who not only do much of the farming but also any number of other heavy tasks — fetching water from the river, collecting firewood from the forests, carrying babies on their backs, cooking and many, many more.

Most people in Kenya and Tanzania would not walk or take exercise in order to lose weight. They are certainly not obsessed with losing weight, sometimes quite the opposite. When I was younger it was generally thought that the fatter you are, the healthier you are. I still hear such comments when I visit family in Africa now. If you are thin, it is assumed that you have a hard life, and people feel sorry for you. On a visit from England to Kenya and Tanzania, I was greeted by a neighbour who, looking very concerned, asked me if I was well. I said I was very well, thank you. She paused. "You look thin. Is your husband taking care of you?" I told her he was taking very good care of me. "He spoils me," I said. "So, why are you so thin? You should be a big lady, especially since you are married to a white man with money." I told her I was perfectly happy the way I am, but I guess she could not understand that someone might actually choose to be thin! Having said that, younger people these days often tend to try to be slim. They are more educated now, and are more aware of the possible health effects of being overweight.

WALKING THE DOG

When I came to England, I was very surprised to see people taking dogs for walks. I had never seen such a thing before! I was even more shocked to see people actually keeping dogs in the house. This was unheard of as far as I was concerned. Some people in Kenya do have dogs, but only to guard the house. The dogs do not live inside the family home but outside, in the family compound, and are fed out there. We don't have freezing winters, perhaps if we did, we would provide them with some kind of shelter, but still this would be outside the house. I have also never seen people in Africa stroking dogs and showing them care and affection. In England, people seem to love their dogs and take them to be part of the family. Maybe you are very fond of pet dogs and cats yourself and think I lack feelings. If that is the case, I don't mean to upset you!

As well as keeping guard dogs, people in Kenya and Tanzania may also have cats. When I was a child, there was always at least one cat around the home. They are allowed inside the house, but only because we want them to catch the rats that eat our stored maize. only to catch rats. You would never see a cat sitting on someone's lap. We simply do not keep pets as the English do.

When we were living in Trowbridge, I once came across an elderly lady pushing a pram with a little dog trotting along beside her. When she got closer, I realised she was taking four little dogs for a walk; or at least, she was going for a walk and four little dogs were accompanying her. The three other dogs were snuggling together inside the pram and only the fourth one was walking, on a lead fastened to the pram. It took me a while to make any sense of what I was seeing. I was thinking that maybe this lady does not have any family and the dogs were her substitute. I wondered what her house must have been like with all these little dogs all over the place. Did she also share her bed with them? When we were living in the Solomon Islands, we knew a couple who allowed their dog to sleep on their bed with them. Perhaps, I thought, it was because they had no children, and their dog was a substitute child.

I once overheard someone say that he loved dogs more than human beings, because dogs are loyal and they never answer back. That may be so, but I love human beings more — even if some people can be a pain in the neck! I do like animals and I hate to see them being treated cruelly, but I would never say I loved them. I love my husband and our children and grandchildren, I like some animals. I prefer cats to dogs, anyway, perhaps as a result of my upbringing. In Kenya, my family were never comfortable with dogs coming close to them or their house. In England, I am slowly getting used to seeing people with pets, and in the village where we live, lots of people have dogs. For some at least the dogs seem to provide company. Quite often when John and I are taking a walk around the village, we meet people with dogs. Sometimes the dog will approach and sniff me, which I am still not comfortable with, but I do my best not to show it. I might even try to stroke the dog — if it is a little one. Our children and grandchildren all have cats and dogs. Who knows, maybe one day I'll have one too!

Before you condemn me for not being as fond of pets as your culture expects me to be, I must confess that we did, in fact, have a pet cat when we lived in Trowbridge. This was not really the result of a choice we made. One day, our eldest daughter, Tuni, came home from university bringing a "present" for us. She told us that a friend of hers had acquired a very young kitten, only to find that her landlord did not allow pets in the house. Tuni then decided that her parents would enjoy having a cat. Our other children were delighted with the creature, so we didn't have the heart to refuse. So, little black-and-white Charlie joined the family, grew up to be big and spoiled black-and-white Charlie, and lived with us for the next eighteen years.

AN UNEXPECTED EFFECT OF THE WEATHER

In England, people are constantly talking about the weather, and I have been surprised to see how it affects their mood. On a nice sunny day, people go around wearing big smiles and are more friendly. When it is a grey day, they are more likely to look gloomy and bad-tempered. When I was working in the NHS, this effect of the weather could sometimes make life difficult if I had to deal with someone whose behaviour was unpredictable. This was a surprise – even a shocked, because I could not understand how anyone can be grumpy about the weather, just because the weather is not what they want it to be! I still find it surprising. I can see how it can be inconvenient, especially if you want to go somewhere and it is pouring with rain, but that's no reason to be grumpy towards others who, after all, didn't make the weather! If the weather is making you feel down or frustrated, why not invite someone for a cup of tea or coffee and a chat?

One of the senior staff nurses at the hospital used to say, "If we are feeling down because of the weather, we still must try to show our warmth to the patients. We should always try to give a smile. It does not cost anything, but it can help a patient feel better when they see a smiling nurse." The same nurse made the following suggestion: "If you are really depressed due to the weather, maybe you should go up to the top of a hill before coming to work, and yell as loudly as you can. See if that helps — then carry on with your journey to work."

I am very proud to say that although in the village where I now live, we do talk about the weather and moan a bit sometimes, no one seems to get grumpy about it. People soon get fed up with talking about the weather, and chat about other things, like their holidays, trips abroad, going sailing... anything positive. Laughter is a great therapy. In my former life, in an African village, talking was probably our main pastime — we chatted all the time, even when we were working.

In Kenya and Tanzania, we did talk about the weather but not in like people do in England. People might be worried if the rains are late, because it affects their livelihoods. In East Africa, people tend to share their smile whatever the weather. Maybe people in Africa don't talk a lot about the weather because it does not change so frequently. (As I write this, we have just had a day here in Derbyshire with high winds, sunshine, heavy rain, hailstones, even snow, all in the space of a few hours!) In East Africa there is a rainy season and a dry season. In the rainy season, most people can be cheerful because the rain allows them to plant their food crops. On the other hand, when the rains do not arrive on time, that does become a point of concern and conversation – it can be a matter of life and death. My cousin Zaina, who lives in Tanzania, tells me that they recently had a severe drought, –more severe than any she has ever experienced. Maybe this is one impact of climate change! It was so bad that you could see the carcasses of wild animals, including elephants, lying about. This made people sad, but not bad-tempered.

TIME AND THE SUN

Arriving in England with my family during wintertime, I was surprised to see the sun set at about four o'clock in the afternoon. People were still at work then! Six months later, I was surprised — but happier — to find that it was still light at almost ten o'clock at night. I found it strange going to bed when it was still light. John explained the change in the length of the days to me, but I still struggled to understand it. I had been taught at school about the Earth travelling around the Sun and spinning on its own axis, etcetera, but it didn't mean much to me, because I had no experience of it. Where I lived, the sun was always high in the sky at midday. Daylight in Kenya came and went at about the same time every day of the year, from about six in the morning to about six in the evening. This is the reason why we count the time of day from six a.m. So, what the English call seven a.m. is, in *Kiswahili,* saa moja asubuhi, or one o'clock in the morning.

What to call a particular time is, however, only a minor cause of misunderstanding when it comes to matters of time. A more significant issue is differences in attitude to time itself. A few years ago, when I was flying to Kenya, I happened to sit next to a couple from England who were heading to Arusha in Tanzania. They were very friendly and we started chatting. The man asked me where I was going to, and I told him I was going to Nairobi and then connecting to another flight to Mombasa. The couple were also going to connect, from Nairobi to Arusha. They told me that they had been to Arusha several times, they loved it and had made friends there. For some reason, we got to talking about time. They said that during their first visit to Arusha, they met an African family from Arusha. Just before the end of their holiday, they arranged to meet this family to have lunch together. They agreed on a day and the time — twelve o'clock. The English couple arrived punctually at twelve. Their friends weren't there, so they waited, and waited... and waited. The family finally arrived at two o'clock in the afternoon. Somewhat to their surprise, the African family offered no apologies and no explanation for why they were so late. As someone from a similar African culture I am sure that, for the family, precise time was not as important as it was for the English couple. Their 'late' arrival was considered neither rude nor in need of an explanation. To them, twelve o'clock (saa sita) meant "around the middle of the day," or even just "lunchtime." Their attitude to life and time was that life was to be taken slowly. An example of this relaxed attitude to life is the way people embark on a journey. If you have to catch a bus, you turn up at the bus stop when you are ready. If you miss one you don't become stressed, you just wait for the next one. It is a bit difficult to take the same approach to catching a plane, however. Flight schedules do not operate according to "African time!"

ENGLISH FOOD

When I came to England, not only did I have to get used to unfamiliar foods, but also to the mealtimes. In rural Africa, we worked in the farm from about nine in the morning to three in the afternoon, without a break. We had a cooked meal after that, when we got home. Friday was our "day off," when we did not go to the fields, so lunch would be eaten earlier, at about one o'clock. Whatever the day, we generally had *sima* (something like polenta) with chicken, beef or fish, or green vegetables. Alternatives to *sima* included cooked green bananas, with or without a stew, or sweet potatoes, yams or maize cobs, on their own. Lunch always included a large portion of carbohydrate of some sort, for the energy we needed to work so hard. In the evening, we would have a second substantial meal. This might be maize seeds cooked with kidney beans, known as puré when the maize seeds have been husked, or boboro if they have not. On special occasions when we had visitors, for instance, we would have chapatis with kidney beans or stew, or perhaps rice with chicken or beef stew. These two meals, lunch and supper, were the main meals of our day.

For breakfast, we would not usually prepare something fresh. When we were cooking on a wood fire and when water had to be fetched from quite a distance away - and not to mention the need to get the cows milked and lots of other early morning tasks – there simply wasn't the time to cook anything complicated. We would have whatever was left over from the previous night's dinner warmed up or, maize-meal porridge. But one thing we had to have before starting our day was freshly-made tea, made the African way with lots of milk, sugar and spices boiled together. If there were no leftovers, we might have to make some *mandazi* (African doughnuts), which are quick to prepare and go well with tea.

In England I was presented with different kinds of meals. Breakfast, I found, was usually cold — some kind of unfamiliar cereal with cold milk. I was also offered a cooked breakfast: oatmeal porridge, toasted bread, bacon or eggs cooked in unfamiliar ways. But there was still tea, even though it was made differently. My mother-in-law always started the day with a cup of tea in bed, a habit which John and I have since adopted.

Lunch was particularly strange to me. Unlike the heavy, cooked meals I was used to in Africa, lunch, I found, was mostly not cooked at all! We would have sandwiches such as cheese and pickle or cheese and tomatoes. Only on a cold day would we have baked potatoes, or baked beans or some other tinned food on toast. After such an English lunch I just did not feel satisfied; I was still hungry and always needed a cup of tea to fill my still-empty stomach. Having tea more than once in a day was an extravagance for me, but I was glad of it. Three cups in a day is now my minimum intake. If drinking tea is seen as an English habit, have I now become English? With electric kettles, water from a tap and a simpler, quicker way of making tea, I can drink as much tea as I want. Although, when I really want to spoil myself, John, or the children, I still sometimes make tea the African way, and cook doughnuts to go with it.

I am now going to discuss the important matter of potatoes! I soon discovered that an English evening meal had to include potatoes in some form. Eating potatoes for supper seemed to be written into English law! The potatoes that are commonly eaten by the English are not the only kind that exist. In Africa, we often eat sweet potatoes and we distinguish these from the potatoes introduced to East Africa by Europeans, which we call 'English potatoes'. We do grow English potatoes in Kenya and Tanzania, but we don't eat them as our main source of carbohydrate, instead they are added to stews, as a vegetable.

Potatoes in England_were cooked in different ways, I discovered, but they were still potatoes, just cooked differently: mashed potatoes with sausages, boiled potatoes with some chicken stew or beef, baked potatoes with baked beans, or chips and chicken nuggets._On a Sunday my in-laws had roast potatoes with roast chicken or beef. I have to admit that I did enjoy the Sunday roast! At Christmas, lunch would be turkey, Brussels sprouts and … roast potatoes. With any other meal, the vegetables always seemed to be either carrots or cabbage, which were always boiled and the cooking water drained into the kitchen sink. This was my very first experience of eating boiled vegetables. I learned later that throwing the vegetable water away is throwing away much of the goodness. To me at the time it seemed that the English could not stay for even a few days without a meal of potatoes. I used to sing to myself, "potatoes, potatoes, potatoes". Maybe it was because the potatoes were cheaper than any other kind of food.

I found this diet rather strange at the time. But after living so many years in England, I think I have now adapted to eating English food - but not potatoes! I have also adapted to eating one cooked meal a day – in the evening - and in the middle of the day I have only a light lunch. Breakfast will usually be porridge and fruits, but not the porridge I used to eat in Kenya (called *uji*), which was made from maize meal with sour milk and some sugar added to it.

For dessert in Kenya, we ate fruits, fresh from our own farm: papayas, pineapples, avocados, guavas, bananas, jackfruits, oranges, pomegranates (very rarely) and mangos — whatever was in season. Bananas were an important part of our diet, coming in all colours and sizes. As well as the bananas like those sold in England, we also have small kisukari bananas, which make a delicious sweet snack at any time. We also have green bananas that do not turn yellow when ripe. The only way to know if such a banana is ready to eat is to give it a gentle squeeze to feel how soft it is. Then we have purple bananas. Even the flesh of these is slightly purple. These are less sweet than the other varieties but are often fatter, making them a more substantial snack. These purple bananas are not my favourite.

I soon noticed that the English peel their bananas starting from the stalk, rather than from the top end, which is where we tend to start. Peeling from the stalk end means you are more likely to squash the banana than when you peel from the opposite end. This is just one of many tiny differences in behaviour (culture) that I encountered.

FURTHER CULTURAL DIFFERENCES

When I began to meet English families, I was shocked to see how some children behaved when they were told off by their parents for having misbehaved. They didn't just answer back, but even shouted at their parents, and in front of visitors too! In Kenya and Tanzania, such behaviour is never condoned. If I did that to my parents, even if there were no visitors present, I would be in deep trouble and my parents would be very angry with me. I would be warned never to answer back nor shout at them ever again. To see such behaviour was totally outside my experience and I really did not know what to make of it at the time. When I think about it now, I realise there were two different things going on here that disturbed me. I was shocked that a child would talk back to his or her parents, and even more so that they did it in front of visitors. Public displays of anger in a family are not acceptable to my upbringing. The other point is that although it was a child that was behaving badly from my point of view, I realise that even I, as a grown-up daughter, would not speak to my parents like that. It is not so much age that matters in this situation but the difference between generations. In Kenya and Tanzania, children are raised to show respect to their elders, whether they are family or not. If a child disagrees with an older person, they must do so calmly and respectfully.

Another thing that surprised me was seeing parents encouraging their small children to take a drink of wine. When I first encountered the parents of a nine-year-old child offering him wine, I asked them why. "Oh," they said, "he only drinks wine at the weekend when we're all together enjoying our Sunday lunch." I still could not digest this answer, and in the end I have resolved it by telling myself that as long as the parents' actions do not hurt me or my children, it is up to them to do what they want when bringing up their children. That does not mean I approve of what I saw but one of the effects on me of living amongst people of other cultures is that I feel I must accept such differences and not interfere. Is this what "tolerance" means, that I must accept what others do, even if it disturbs me?

I could hardly believe my ears when, soon after coming to England, I heard children addressing adults by their first name. In East Africa, this is unacceptable, a sign of utter disrespect. Later, I came to understand that this form of address is just another cultural difference.

As for us, we are trained from a very early age that as soon as you get up in the morning, the first thing you must do is greet your parents, by saying "*Shikamoo*." This literally means "I kiss your feet.", but of course, we don't really kiss anybody's feet! It is just a respectful way for young people to greet their parents and other elders. An older person never says "*Shikamoo*" to someone younger than them. Adult visitors are also greeted with "*Shikamoo*," followed by a handshake (remembering always to use the right hand) and a bow. This greeting is obligatory if the visitor is an important personage — the village chief, perhaps, or the local headmaster. If the visitor is an Imam, the greeting is, "*Asalaam alaykum*." Women, however, do not shake hands with an Imam.

HOUSING

I found it rather unusual that people in England didn't seem to mind moving into a house that other people had lived in before them. In Kenya and Tanzania, no one ever considered occupying a "second-hand" house. Fancy moving into a place that smelled of other people's cooking, and their woodsmoke — horrible! At the same time, people in the villages do not sell their houses because the land on which it is built is where they grow their food, and is passed down from generation to generation. It is also where one's forebears are buried, whose spirits inhabit that land. A family in dire straits might sell some of their land, but not that on which their home is built.

There were no building restrictions in the villages, no planning permission was required. You could build your house however you liked. The only exceptions are the lands belonging to plantations or other large companies. Near where I grew up there was a large sisal plantation, with rows of identical houses for the workers. These houses did not belong to the occupiers, however, and they would only be temporary homes until they changed their jobs. In urban areas today in Kenya and Tanzania, housing regulations do apply and housing estates comprising rows of identical houses have been built. Unlike the villages, where houses tend to be more scattered rather than in rows, urban housing is built in lines along the sides of roads. These houses are often built for renting by people who work in the city, who will generally have land and a house back 'home' and to which they will return as often as they can.

Brassington village, where we now live, lies within what is called a conservation area. I did not really understand what this meant until we had been living here for a while. Basically, it means that there are restrictions on what residents can and cannot do with their houses and gardens. For example, when we decided that our outside window frames needed repainting, we were told that we weren't allowed to paint them in whatever colour we liked. We found a deep blue colour that we rather fancied, but one of our neighbours told us we weren't permitted to use that colour, and we had to look for an alternative one that would fit in with the rest of the village. On another occasion, we wanted to remove a scruffy laburnum tree from the garden and get our maple tree trimmed, and we had to obtain permission from the District Council to do it. I couldn't believe it! Imagine having to get permission to cut down a dying tree in your own garden. Ridiculous! John tried to explain the reasoning behind this, but to this day, I am still puzzled. Nevertheless, despite these restrictions, I am happy to be a part of this village.

CHILDREN AT PLAY

I was surprised to find that English parents accompany their children to the playground, even when they are old enough to go by themselves. I discovered later that there are people around who cannot be trusted with children, paedophiles who might abduct or harm them. I had never heard of adults deliberately abusing children. Growing up in rural villages in Kenya, we were free-range children, playing where we liked, and no one ever tried to harm us.

Also, there was no place designated as a playground, except for the school compound, which we never went to because it was too far. The smaller children played within the family compound — not for fear of adults with bad intentions, but in case they fought with each other. It seems that children everywhere tend to squabble and fight! In the rural villages the area surrounding the home was large enough for children to play and even kick a football about.

When we first lived in England, John and I had to take our four children to the playground if they wanted to get out, because the garden was too small. They also loved having a place with swings and a slide and other things for them to play on. They did know about swings before that because, outside our house in Kenya, we had made a swing for them from a length of rope and an old car tyre, but they found the English swings more exciting. But we were constantly having to keep an eye on the children wherever they were, to make sure they were safe. I found this hard work. We felt that we should not trust anyone apart from family members or friends or neighbours. This was very sad but I also found it frightening that there were sinister people around who might do them harm. The only time I could relax was when they were inside the house watching television or playing together. Perhaps, I thought, this is why most people in England only have one or two children.

I became doubly wary about safety when I found out that some people, especially older people, had a chain on the inside of their front door that would allow it to be opened only a small distance. If someone knocked on the door, it would be opened a little way, just enough to allow the inhabitant to see who it was. Only if the visitor is known and trusted, is the chain detached and they can enter. I had never come across this in my Kenyan village life.

HOLDING HANDS

One thing that I really admired when I came to England was people holding hands when walking together. I found it really sweet. In most African cultures, especially in my time in Kenya and Tanzania, couples or friends, would not openly display affection in that way. It is considered indecent; and as for kissing in public — that is absolutely taboo. The very first time I held hands with John was in Tamworth, in early 1985, when we were going to town to do some shopping. I distinctly remember him taking my hand when we reached a corner just before the shopping centre. That's how memorable it was! I did feel a bit shy because I was not accustomed to showing affection in public. Nowadays, we can easily hold each other's hands; it feels natural, and we know there will be no bad comments from people in the streets. Even in Kenya and Tanzania now, couples sometimes do hold hands, but only in the big towns and cities, never in the villages.

AGE

After a few years of living in England, I learnt that you must never ask a woman how old she is. In Kenya and Tanzania, people are perfectly happy to disclose their age, and are never offended if they are asked. On one occasion, an English friend of mine invited me to accompany her and her mother to town. It was a sunny day, and she wanted to look at the shops and visit the market, since it was market day. Later on, she suggested we go for a coffee or tea. The three of us headed towards the town centre, with my friend's sixty-eight-year-old mother, who knew the town well, in the lead. Following behind, my friend called out, "Keep your head up, Mum, you're bent forward like an old lady." For me, at the age of twenty-eight, it was a surprise that my friend's mother should not want to be seen as an old lady. I nearly said, "But your mother is old!" Thinking that might be impolite on my part, however, I said nothing, but I was surprised that a sixty-eight-year-old woman should not want to be seen as 'old'. Then I remembered that back home, you are considered old at fifty. When my father reached the age of fifty, he said he was lucky to have lived so long and especially to have lived to see his grandchildren. He said this because some of his friends had died before they reached that age. My father eventually died at the age of eighty-five, and we all miss him very much.

FIREWORK NIGHT

The first time I saw a fireworks display was in Tamworth in 1985. The children and I were fascinated, apart, that is, from Nurudin, who was very young at the time. He was terrified. We were amazed at the different colours and the patterns they made in the night sky, and the fizzing, popping sounds they made. Everyone was enjoying the show, cheering when the next one went up. It was a very exciting evening that I still remember clearly, thirty-seven years later. Many years after this first experience, we were living in China and fireworks were a common sight: when it is someone's birthday, there are fireworks; when someone has opened a new shop, fireworks; and when someone has died — if they are Buddhists — there are fireworks (together with a brass band and drums).

We saw plenty of Buddhist funerals, because we lived in a twentieth-floor flat in the city of Ningbo, and there was a temple just below us. We were often startled out of our sleep at the crack of dawn by fireworks exploding, followed by the noise of the band as a funeral procession left the temple. If we managed to get back to sleep after this rude awakening, we would be woken again about twenty minutes later when the band returned.

Chinese New Year was the occasion for the biggest firework displays, which went on all night and long into the following day. Sleep was in short supply during these celebrations! We discovered later that Ningbo was unusual in this respect, as many major Chinese cities, for reasons of safety, had limited the use of fireworks to officially organised public displays. Chinese New Year's Eve could be a wild time in Ningbo. I remember walking back home from a dinner with friends just as it turned midnight. The sky went crazy with explosions. It looked and sounded like a war zone, except that everyone was happy and excited. Amid gales of laughter, the people around us called out, "Xin nian kuaile!" (Happy New Year). This was quite a contrast with the normally quiet streets. The crowd was loud and boisterous, but in contrast to England, we saw no drunken behaviour, and we always felt perfectly safe.

GARDENS

I was very impressed when I first came to England to see how people kept their gardens, so well laid-out in lovely patterns and full of flowers of different colours. "These people are creative and knowledgeable," I thought. When I was out walking, I could not stop looking at the gardens I passed, and the way the flowers were arranged. I still enjoy looking at gardens, it makes me smile, and I am sure many other people feel the same way too. Even more amazing was that it is not just people's home gardens that received such loving care but also public spaces, the grounds of castles and even the roundabouts and roadside verges. I even came across place names that were spelt out in flowers. I was also struck by how clean and tidy the streets and gardens were.

Living here in Derbyshire, I have become an "English-style" gardener myself, and I really enjoy planting flowers and shrubs, just for the way they look. I always had been a "gardener" when I lived in Kenya, but that was gardening for food not flowers for beauty. I must say, however, they may have taken this woman out of Africa, but they haven't taken Africa out of this woman. In amongst the flowers I still plant my maize, beans and cabbage!

CLEANLINESS AND TIDINESS

In September 2022, I had a two-week holiday in Kenya and Tanzania with Mani and his wife, Umi. Arriving in Mombasa, the first thing that struck us was how dirty and messy the streets were, littered with plastic bottles, plastic bags and other kinds of rubbish. The sides of the roads were strewn with used nappies, broken utensils, old sacks, torn clothes, banana skins, sugar cane waste, all apparently tossed out of the windows of passing vehicles. The main problem is that the local councils do not provide rubbish bins; but also, people have not been educated about how to dispose of waste in public spaces. We are very careful to keep our own premises clean but there is an attitude that public spaces are "somebody else's problem". England is not at all perfect in this respect but it is no comparison to what I saw in Kenya.

People in the rural villages of Kenya sweep their compounds nearly every day. This was especially important for us when we had cows and goats that leave their droppings as they come out from their fenced-in holding area. Most importantly, this keeps the flies at bay. When my mother-in-law first visited us in Kenya, she said she had expected to find flies everywhere; this was the image of Africa portrayed on TV — images of children with flies crawling over their faces. In fact, my mother-in-law said, she had seen more flies at an English picnic than she saw in Kenya.

If I were still living in a Kenyan or Tanzanian town, it is more than likely that I, too, would have been littering the streets just like everyone else. Living in England I learned not to throw rubbish anywhere but in the bins that are provided and to be more aware of my surroundings. I believe that education is the key to making people aware of the importance of keeping the environment free of rubbish. It looks better for a start, but more importantly, it is hygienic.

WASHING THE DISHES

You may wonder why I should bother writing about such a trivial thing as doing the washing-up. Surely, you may be asking, people all over the world wash the dishes the same way. Not so! When I came to England, I found that even this everyday activity was done quite differently. For a start, I was surprised to see people washing their dishes in a bowl of soapy water and not rinsing them off with clean water afterwards. When I saw this, I assumed there was a shortage of water, and was surprised to find this wasn't so. It is an English habit that I have never adopted.

My point is that "culture" is not just a matter of things like art or religion, or music or even the way we dress, it is also about how we live our everyday lives. My initial interpretation of the dish-washing behaviour that I saw was that a lack of water must be the reason for it. In the villages, in the past anyway, water was not something we lacked but something we had to work hard to fetch, and that made us more careful in how we used it.

I am happy to say that people in the village of Usangi now have access to running water. It is still not available in the houses, but from a communal tap outside. This is still a whole lot better than having to fetch water from the river almost a mile away, with a heavy bucket on your head coming back. There is electricity too, used for lights, television and radios - and recently for charging mobile phones, which have not just changed behaviour in Africa but have become a necessity of life. That is what I mean by a cultural change.

Those of my extended family in Kenya who live in a big city or town have electricity and running water in their houses. Some, such as my niece, Zania, have a washing machine, although I don't think anyone has a dishwasher. Washing clothes by hand is hard work and takes a long time, washing dishes by hand is much easier! Washing clothes by hand dries your skin too. This is not trivial: one of my family members worked as a washerwoman, washing clothes for other families, and her skin became so rough, damaged and discoloured that she was embarrassed when she had to shake hands – which is a very important part of our culture.

SWIMMING

The first time I swam in the cold British sea was in 1985, when John, his mother and I took the children to Nefyn, on the Lleyn Peninsula in North Wales. It was my very first holiday, as well as the first time I slept in a caravan — I'd never even seen one before then. The children were too young then to remember this holiday now. John and I decided we would try to go for an early morning swim each day, leaving the children with Mum. I jumped straight into the sea, thinking it would be warm like the Indian Ocean. How wrong I was! It was so cold it took my breath away. I came up gasping. I think John found it a shock as well, and we didn't stay long in the water. Afterwards, we ran along the sand together, and arrived back at the caravan with our bodies glowing. In Nefyn I also ate, for the first time, the traditional English dish of battered fish and chips with vinegar. I liked it, but nowadays I avoid the vinegar and I like to unpack the fish from inside the batter and eat just the steamed fish that is left, which I guess is not the "proper" way to eat it.

The train journey to Nefyn was the longest I had made in Britain. I was delighted by the green, rolling hills and the fields full of fat, woolly sheep, which are nothing like African sheep. I was surprised to learn that the sheep were left unattended in the fields, even at night. Did no one steal them? The last part of the journey took us along the Dovey estuary and the edge of the sea. Even now, John and I still try to repeat that journey when we can – such as by visiting John's brother and his wife, who live in West Wales. I still enjoy walking in those lovely hills with their view of the deep blue sea. Perhaps it was this holiday that changed the opinion I had had of "going for a walk" as being a waste of time – 'Had I no work to do?'

I have lived and travelled now in many different countries and I have come to accept and welcome cultural differences. "Tradition" is good, so long as it does not hurt anyone. The world would be a boring place if we were all alike and did things in exactly the same way. I believe that in the end we humans all want the same things — to be loved and respected, and to live together in peace and harmony, whatever our colour or culture.

Chapter 3

The Solomon Islands

Those of you who have read my first book might be wondering why I am again writing about the Solomon Islands. This is because in my first book I did not write as much as I could have done, especially since I enjoyed our life there so much. Indeed, some readers may not know where the Solomon Islands are or have only a vague idea, such as "somewhere in the Pacific." Even the person who interviewed me for BBC Radio Derby said that he didn't know where the Solomon Islands were — he had to go and check on the map. To be honest, so did we!

The Solomon Islands are indeed "in the Pacific"; a string of islands a few hundred miles north-east of Australia. John got a job there after completing his Master's degree. Although I did not know much at all about the country or even the Pacific Ocean when we set off, my time living in Honiara, the capital of the Solomons, turned out to be one of those experiences I will always treasure.

We arrived in Honiara in January, 1987. Coming out of the aeroplane was like walking into a bowl of hot soup. I wondered how we would survive in such heat. We got used to the climate, however, and even came to love it. We quickly adapted to wearing very light clothes, as everyone else did. There was none of the nonsensical wearing of suits and ties in order to be "smart" no matter how hot it is, as in East Africa, and it was a big change from England, where we had grown used to wearing multiple layers of clothing to keep warm. Despite the heat, I wouldn't have minded spending the rest of my life in the Solomons. The only downside was the mosquitoes, but coming from Kenya, I was used to them.

The people we met were so friendly, they smiled easily and always had time for a chat. I appreciated this about them, because I love meeting, talking and sharing with people. I would not be happy living somewhere with beautiful views and warm weather if the people were unfriendly. People are the most important part of my life, maybe because I was brought up in a large family and I always had lots of people around me.

Honiara is a port on the coast of the island of Guadalcanal. The island is mountainous, the slopes covered in thick green jungle. Many rivers and smaller streams flow down from these hills to the sea, often forming impressive waterfalls. There were plenty of wonderful walks, but it was essential to have someone with us who knew where they were going, as it would have been easy to get lost in the thick jungle. We would pass through deep forests, walking through rivers and even sometimes using a river as a path for a while. When it is so warm and you are soaked with sweat anyway, walking into a river is a great way to cool off. We just plunged in with our clothes on. If we were feeling really hot, we would sit in the river to relax and get cool, or find a deeper pool to swim in. Many of our walks ended at a waterfall deep in the forest, where we would sit under the deep blue sky eating our picnic and admiring the view. After a long walk in the jungle, we would finish off with a final plunge in a river before returning home. I have to admit that I have swum in one of these wonderful rivers when I was wearing nothing - but I only dared to do this when I was just walking with John. Swimming naked for the first time in my life felt strange but such an amazing experience at the same time. I experienced a mixture of lightness and freedom. If you have ever done it, you will know what I mean. After the way I had been brought up, it took a lot of courage to do this for the first time.

We often took the children with us on these jungle walks, and they loved it. Nurudin, our younger son, first learned to swim in a river in the middle of a tropical jungle! Nurudin always swam with his eyes open, which made them sore, but he said he wanted to see what was underneath the water and did not feel comfortable with his eyes shut. One of the good things about walking in the jungle in the Solomon Islands was that it was safe; there were no dangerous animals and no dangerous snakes.

There were places in the forest that the Islanders regarded as sacred and to which foreigners were not allowed to go. Legend has it that many, many years ago a white man unknowingly wandered into one of these sacred places and was killed, cooked and eaten.

Guadalcanal, along with the other islands we visited had stunning beaches, sandy and edged with palm trees. We took our children swimming most weekends, loading up an *esky* with plenty of cold drinks, sandwiches and fruit. (*Esky* is the Australian name for a cool-box; people in Honiara used a lot of Australian expressions). The children would spend the day happily, building sand castles, playing with pebbles or chasing each other in games of tag. They learned to snorkel there and our eldest, Tuni, even went on to do some scuba diving.

There was one beach, called Bonegi 1, that John and I often used to take the children to. It was not far away, but what was special about it was that there was a wrecked ship just below the surface of the sea off the shore. This was a Japanese supply ship which was sunk by the Americans during the battle for control of Guadalcanal. It was one of many relics from World War II to be found on the island or in the seas around it: ships, aeroplanes, tanks, even a submarine. When we were there, a lot of Japanese tourists used to come to visit the battlefields and the striking, very moving Japanese war memorial on a hill overlooking Honiara.

This shipwreck made Bonegi 1 very popular with divers and snorkellers. You could see so many different types of coral and many-coloured fish which had no fear of humans — probably because the swimmers sometimes fed them. Even though I am not a confident swimmer, I was tempted to try snorkelling there, and found it truly beautiful. On one occasion, I was snorkelling over the wreck with John when suddenly I was faced with a sheer drop over the edge of the vessel. Looking down into the deep blue nothingness of the ocean, I panicked and splashed back to the beach, leaving John behind. Who knew what might be down there! Mainly, I was thinking of sharks. There are quite a lot of sharks around the Solomon Islands, but they mostly keep away from the shore. One day, we did see a dead shark at Bonegi that had been swept ashore. It was enough to keep me from doing any more diving. I preferred to spend my time relaxing on the beach or playing in the shallower water with the children.

Some people just went to the beach to relax and read a book in the shade of the palm trees. It was always warm and humid in the Solomons, but at least at the beach there was usually a breeze. Not that people talked much about the weather or worried about it — except when the occasional storm blew in — because the weather was always the same; sunshine and blue skies. This reminded me of Africa, where the sun always shines, except in the rainy season, which doesn't last very long. Sometimes we would see strangely shaped clouds in the sky above Honiara. One I particularly remember was exactly like a bird's feather, down to the last detail. It appeared just over our house, and it looked so real I felt I could reach up, pluck it from the sky and tickle someone under the chin with it.

Sometimes at the weekend we would get up very early in the morning and take the children to the beach to have breakfast there, before the sun got too hot. As a special treat we would stop at the bakery and pick up some hot, fresh-out-of-the-oven buns filled with cream, which the children loved. (They weren't the only ones!) The children had the time of their lives living in the Solomons and they made lots of friends, some of whom they are still in touch with. It was a great place to bring up children; we did not have to worry about them when they were playing outside. They were "free-range" children and we knew no one would harm them.

Having a barbecue on the beach was another practice that we happily picked up from Australian friends. On at least one occasion, we had a barbecued Christmas dinner on the beach. Another time, we went with John's students to have an end-of-term barbecue on the beach, and it poured with rain. It rained so heavily that the chicken and fish barbecue turned into a stew. After an hour or so, the students decided it was warmer to sit in the sea than on the beach. They still enjoyed their day out, though. When I was a child in Kitoghoto village, I used to go outside in the rain in my underwear and dance in the rain, singing away happily in *Kipare*.

We used to meet an Australian man and his family at the beach, and his two children played with ours. He was remarkable in that he kept baby crocodiles in a hole in the ground just outside his house. The crocodiles were only young, but crocodiles of any age or size because they remind me of a relative of mine who was eaten by a crocodile when she and her friends were washing clothes in the river. She was only twelve. The Australian man said he only kept the crocodiles for a short time and then released them into the river. I was very pleased to see that the hole in the ground had a heavy lid on it!

I would love to go back to the Solomons, but at the

same time I know that if I did, I might well be disappointed. We move on and change, and so do the places we have lived in. I have such happy memories of that time, and I would not like them spoiled by the changes I know have taken place there since we left. Memories of places cannot be separated from the time in which they were experienced — the time of my life, of our family life and just the time of the world.

I have lost contact with almost everyone that I knew in the Solomons, but I am very fortunate to still have my friend, Tino Fradd, who is from Western Samoa. Like us, she and her English husband, Mike, returned to settle in England. Tino is a special kind of person; the kind that is good for you! I cannot be in Tino's company for more than a minute without ending up in fits of laughter. Tino carries sunshine around with her.

HONIARA MARKET

I have been told that over seventy different languages are spoken in the Solomon Islands. Each island is home to many languages. That being so, Pidgin English (or just 'pijin' as it is generally called) is spoken by most people when faced with a multi-lingual situation. Being the capital city, Honiara attracts people from all islands in the archipelago but if you were to ask someone living in Honiara where she is from, she would probably name the island where she was born and brought up, or where her extended family still lives. People retain the identity and the language of their 'home' island. For example, the lady who helped me with the housework was from Makira, a large island south-east of Honiara. A lot of the inhabitants of Honiara were originally from the island of Malaita to the east. Malaitans are known as the business-people of the Solomons, and have the reputation of being rather aggressive and domineering. In contrast, the people from Santa Isabel, a large island to the north-west of Honiara, are considered to be more gentle.

People in all of the islands grow staple crops, such as cassava, sweet potatoes, yams, sweet corn, coconuts and bananas. They grow a wide range of vegetables, including cabbage, okra, spinach, runner beans, spring cabbage, slippery cabbage, aubergines, onion and spring onions. Other vegetables imported from Australia were sold in the supermarkets, carrots being one that I remember because we used to eat a lot of them, although the Solomon Islanders tended not to. The ship from Australia that brought the imported foods only came about once a month. We used to buy plenty of carrots because we did not know when the ship would come next. Someone advised us that the best way to keep carrots fresh for longer was to individually wrap them in newspaper and keep them in the fridge; and indeed they did last much longer that way.

We would buy most of our vegetables in the open-air market by the sea, as well as the local fruits, such as papayas, pineapples, mangos, bananas, lemons and limes. We freshly squeezed lemons nearly every day to make a refreshing drink; in the heat of Honiara, we had to remember to drink a lot to remain hydrated and it was nicer to have cold lemon juice to hand, rather than plain water. We would also buy fish at this market, which we kept in an *esky*, and which were often so recently caught that they were still wriggling.

The market stalls were covered to keep direct sunlight off the produce and the seller, but open-sided to allow the cooling sea breeze through. Under these shelters, the sellers placed empty sacks or fresh banana leaves on the ground, and arranged their fruit and vegetables on them. A few had more substantial wooden kiosks with a counter and shelves. The whole market set-up was so familiar to me. It reminded me of Taveta market, where my aunt Khadija and I used sell the woven baskets we had made.

Tino and I would drive to the market in the early morning before it became too hot, so as to buy our vegetables, fruits and fish while they were fresh. When we had done our shopping there, she would drive me to another open market about five minutes away, also by the sea. This market specialised in fresh fish and crabs which were barbecued on the spot. The two markets were separate because the smoke from the barbecues might irritate the fruit and vegetable sellers. As well as barbecued seafood, we could also get roasted cassava there. Tino would park the car and we would queue to buy some barbecued tuna and salted roasted cassava. We would then find a shady place to sit facing the sea. With the sunshine and deep blue skies, it was truly idyllic. We would eat our fresh barbecue, smile at each other and say, "Aren't we lucky to be here!" Watching the waves breaking on the shore was very relaxing, it was like being on holiday. In fact, just being in the Solomons was a holiday in itself. The times I spent sitting there with Tino eating our local barbecue were very special, and I will never forget them.

They are moments that will stay with me for the rest of my life.

We were in no rush to get home, and we stayed out as long as we could. The only thing we had to get back for was to pick up our children from school. Life in the Solomon Islands was taken slowly, just as it was in Kenya and Tanzania. Time was of little consequence. If you didn't finish what you were doing today, there was always tomorrow! In England, people are always conscious of the time, everything must be done this minute, and it can be very stressful.

Traditional Dancing in the Solomons

In the Solomons, events are always celebrated with traditional dancing. At King George VI School, where John was teaching, there was an annual dancing competition. This was an important event and was taken very seriously by the students, who would practice for weeks beforehand. I liked watching the dances, although I didn't know much about what they signified. In the school competition, the dancers were judged on their performance, but also on whether the dance was sufficiently "traditional." When they danced, the boys wore rough hessian skirts tied at the waist. Around their ankles were strings of hollow nut shells, tied together loosely so that they rattled in time with the music as they stamped their feet. They painted white patterns on their faces and bodies, which showed up starkly against their brown skin, especially in the evening light. Holding wooden spears and basketwork shields, they danced around each other to the beat of a wooden slit drum hollowed out from a fallen tree trunk. The girls, whose faces were also painted, all wore long raffia skirts and beadwork around their foreheads, arms and bodies.

In the KGVI dance competition there was also a separate dance, which did not form part of the competition. This followed a dancing style brought to the Solomon Islands from Kiribati (formerly known as the Gilbert Islands when it was a British Colony). There was a Kiribati community in Honiara, and in other parts of the Solomons too, who had brought their customs with them when they were driven from Kiribati by drought and other pressures. The people of Kiribati are Micronesian, while the Solomon Islanders are almost all Melanesian. The Micronesians are generally lighter-skinned than the Melanesians, and have straighter hair. The dances performed by the Kiribati girls mostly involve swaying and movement of the hips, whereas the Melanesian girl dancers move their feet more. We enjoyed all of the dances, whoever was performing!

One year, our two sons, Mani and Nurudin, were invited to participate with the students in these traditional dances. They had a marvellous life in the Solomons and being included in the dancing was one of the high points of their time there. Over thirty years later they still have wonderful memories that they spontaneously share with each other, often coming out with *pijin* expressions that they find fit certain situations better than English or *Kiswahili*. For example, in the appropriate situation they find "Yu filim nao!" much more meaningful than "Now you know how it feels!" They will also use *pijin* in private conversations in the midst of a crowd, assuming no one will understand. John and I occasionally use *Kiswahili* for the same purpose, but there are times when we have been caught out!

Flowers in the Solomons

When we came to the Solomon Islands, one thing we noticed immediately was that there were flowers everywhere. There were hedges of bougainvillaea in shades of red, pink, white, and orange. Turning our gaze from the bougainvillaea, we would be delighted by rows of brilliant red hibiscus. In gardens or in public spaces, there were glorious frangipani trees with their beautiful white flowers tinged with yellow, their delicate perfume carried by the breeze as we passed them. Along the main road into Honiara were stands of the flamboyant trees that we were used to seeing in East Africa, where they are known as Christmas trees because their brilliant red flowers appear at that time.

With so many flowers around, they were the natural choice for decorating venues where a special event was being held. At the end of the school year at King George VI School, the students would spend an entire day making complicated and spectacular arrangements of flowers on palm leaves. Garlands of flowers were hung around the necks of arriving or departing visitors. We wore these when we left the Solomon Islands for the last time — a delightful gesture on an otherwise sad occasion.

Young women would often wear a hibiscus flower in their hair, usually behind one ear. A friend of mine from Makira told me what it meant. Apart from being decorative, it sent a message to any potential admirer. If the flower was worn on the righthand side of the head, it meant the wearer was married and therefore unavailable. A flower behind the left ear meant, "I am single, and available." As for a flower worn on the top of the head, the message – so I was told - was "It depends who's asking..."

Needless to say, the men didn't have an equivalent symbol!

EXPATRIATE WIVES

Most wives of expatriate workers – including me - were not permitted to work, according to our husbands' contracts, so we had to find ways to pass the time. Having time on my hands was a new experience for me. In Kenya, as I have said, there was always more than enough to be done and in England I was a busy housewife and mother. In the Solomons, the children were all at school and I had help in the house. I needed to find something to do that would give me a chance to meet new people and make friends.

Many expatriate wives were involved in sporting activities, such as aerobics, tennis and squash. I tried them all and quite enjoyed the aerobics and squash. A group of us decided we would like to get together for activities other than sport that would help us get to know each other by sharing something of our different backgrounds. We decided on cooking. The idea was to get together to share our traditional foods and how to cook them. It would help us to get to know each other better, which was what we really wanted to do.

We decided that each of us would cook a traditional dish from our country and bring it to share with the others, along with the recipe if anyone was interested. We would meet once a month. It was a great idea, but where could we hold the meetings? We were a big group — around fifty women. Someone suggested that perhaps those with larger houses could offer themselves as hosts. Luckily, four women generously offered to open their homes to us. The first house we went to was that of an English lady I hadn't met before.

On the appointed day, I pulled up outside her house and carried my traditional dish up to the front door. My first impression was, "Wow! What a beautiful house!" Inside, I found that some people had already arrived. I said hello to everyone and put my contribution on the dining room table along with the other meals. Every food was labelled to say, what the food was, what the ingredients were and which country it came from. In the sitting room, everyone was talking away happily, and there was a pleasant atmosphere.

Outside, the sunshine and blue skies added to the feeling that today's meeting would go well. Inside the house the rooms all seemed so spacious, especially compared to my house! We introduced ourselves, giving our name and the country we came from. I thought the lady of the house looked rather posh, going by the clothes she wore, her large house and the way she carried herself. I discovered later that her husband was the First Secretary of the British High Commission.

When everyone had arrived, we decided it was time to help ourselves to the food. With fifty people each bringing something, there was a huge amount of food to choose from. We each helped ourselves and returned to the sitting room to eat, sitting on any chair or cushion that was available. I knew some of the women from the aerobics classes, others knew each other from tennis or other activities. People would tend to sit with others with whom they felt comfortable, which often meant people they already knew.

I had brought a dish of *sima* (maize meal), spinach and beef. I had cheated a bit, because the beef was made from a West African recipe, with peanut butter added, which we would not do in East Africa. The others liked the beef stew, but not the *sima* which wasn't a surprise to me. *Sima* is generally only appreciated by Africans, and eaten on its own it doesn't have much flavour (then again, neither has rice). Another reason why the others did not like it was that *sima* has to be eaten with your hands, which must be washed very well with clean water before starting. That was already a complication for most people who were not used to eating with their hands – perhaps especially those who came from a more "superior" background. If I love *sima,* and eating with my bare hands, does this mean I cannot be superior?

SOCIAL STATUS

The women in this group came from many different countries — the United Kingdom, Australia, New Zealand, Fiji, India, the Netherlands, Ireland, Sri Lanka, Tanzania, Kenya, to name but a few - and not forgetting the locals of Honiara, the Solomon Islanders. We all enjoyed tasting the foods from our different countries. There were differences in culture, too, but that did not seem to matter and we all got on well.

I soon discovered, however, that in the world of the expatriate, a woman's social identity was based on her husband's occupation. This meant that I was ranked among the lower social orders, since my husband was "only" a secondary school teacher, while many of the other women's husbands were engineers, doctors, diplomats, and so on. This discovery on my part on the rules governing status came about in the following way.

Our English hostess had cooked a very nice meal of fish. It was really tasty and many of the women said it was the best of the lot. I liked it very much too. A woman I knew called Jane, however, was less than impressed. She asked me in a whisper who had made it. She had arrived late and did not know the woman whose house it was. I pointed her out to Jane: "That woman over there." The woman overheard me, and snapped, "How dare you call me a woman! I am a lady. My husband is the First Secretary of the British High Commission." I felt obliged to apologise.

Later, I told John about this. His response was, "So now we know who her husband is, but who is she?" He was right; what did she do, other than be a housewife, like the rest of us. Nevertheless, I am now careful not to call someone a woman, but to always say "lady."

TRAVELS AROUND THE SOLOMON ISLANDS

John was always saying we should visit some of the other islands while we were in Honiara. After all, we weren't going to be there forever, and we should use the opportunity while we could. So, during the school holidays we visited some of the many islands that make up the Solomons. Two that I particularly remember are the Reef Islands and Q Island. In those days, the Solomon Islands wasn't a tourist destination, although we discovered so many fantastic places to visit. Cruise ships occasionally visited Honiara for a few days (often leaving a new flu virus behind that we local residents had no immunity to), some came for the scuba-diving, and a few Japanese tourists visited the WWII sites, but that was all.

We decided to go to the Reef Islands first. These are a group of small islands two or three hundred miles to the south-east of Guadalcanal, with a vast expanse of sea between them and Honiara. It was this remoteness that tempted us to visit them. We flew from Honiara Airport, still called Henderson Field, the name the Americans gave it during World War II. To get to the Reef Islands, we first had to fly to Lata on Santa Cruz Island, which was the nearest airfield to the Reef islands themselves. The aeroplane was very small and the flight was very bumpy and my hands were sweating, as they do when I am nervous. But John and the children enjoyed the flight, and the children thought going up and down in the air was great fun.

We landed safely at Lata airfield. A notice on the wall of the sole corrugated iron airport building declared this was

'Lata International Airport', dating – I was told - from the time when there were flights from there to Vanuatu. Here we met Bresson who was waiting to take us to our destination. He was the son of the couple who owned the 'resort' in the Reef Islands. He helped us carry our luggage to the harbour where his boat was moored. The boat turned out to be of the same design as the majority of those found around the islands – an open fibre-glass boat with an outboard motor. It was just big enough to carry us, along with Bresson and two other men. I should point out that the Reef Islands are about twenty or so miles from Lata across the open sea!

I was a bit apprehensive, especially after our bumpy flight, at the prospect of crossing the open sea in this small vessel. I am not a good sailor, I get nervous, but John and the children were all looking forward to it. All went well (apart from what seemed to me to be rough sea) until, about an hour before the Reef Islands, the boat ran out of fuel! What a disaster, I thought. First the bumpy flight and now the boat has run out of fuel in the middle of the sea. What next! Bresson said that he and the two men would have to row the boat for the last few miles. John looked at me and said nothing; maybe he did not want to say anything in front of the children. The sea was getting rougher, but Bresson didn't seem to be worried. I imagined that he was used to these things happening. Anyway, we got there in the end. Phew!

As we got out of the boat, Bresson's mother came to welcome us. She showed us to our chalet, which had three bedrooms and a thatched roof. She was curious to know where we came from, probably because it was so unusual, especially in this remote spot to see a black lady with a white man. John always finds it harder than I do to answer this question. Born in Bristol, he moved to Durham and then to Tamworth, then spent twelve years in Kenya before returning to Tamworth, and now he lives in the Solomon Islands. "Where should I say I am from?" he will ask. (I get cross with him when he says that because he really does know what the person is asking about!)

Bresson's mother had said her son would be happy to take us out fishing if we wanted to go. However, the day after our arrival, we decided against it. After the previous day's crossing, it was the last thing I wanted to do. Instead, we decided to explore the island. Nearing the shore, we spotted another island about a mile away. Bresson said he would be happy to take us there in his boat, so we set off after lunch. It wasn't far, but I was still nervous going by boat again after our experience of the day before. The island turned out to be bigger than the one we were staying on and there were more people around. We took the children to the beach, where they played barefoot in the white sand, and joined other children in building sandcastles. John and I sat with a drink in the shade of the palm trees, watching the local people messing about in their boats and calling out to passers-by to take a boat trip or go fishing.

Out in the islands the air felt fresher than we had become used to in Honiara, even though we had never thought of it as being polluted. This was partly because there were no cars, and the only means of transport was a boat. John and I wandered along the shoreline, playing with the children and just enjoying the sunshine. We could not have asked for a better place to take a holiday. This trip is one of many that we will always treasure.

After a week on the Reef islands, it was time to go back to Honiara for Christmas. Then, the day before we were due to return, a cyclone passed through the area, bringing very heavy rains and high winds, and leaving the sea even rougher than ever. To catch our flight home, we had to take the long journey across the sea to Santa Cruz. Bresson's mother told us that it was too dangerous to undertake the crossing just then. Apparently, a few years earlier, a couple staying on the island had insisted on being taken back in similar weather conditions, and their boat had capsized, drowning them. There was nothing for it but to stay for another two days, when one of the ships that provide inter-island contact, the *Kirsten M,* was due to call on Christmas Eve and we could take that to Santa Cruz.

The ship arrived and we travelled back to Lata overnight. On these inter-island ships, there are usually a few cabins, although most people preferred to sleep out on the open deck. In this case there was just one cabin that was small and rather stuffy, so we opted to sleep out on deck. We were almost the only passengers, apart from some pigs which "Oinked" loudly all night. We arrived on Santa Cruz on Christmas morning, not sure where we would stay or whether we would find anything to eat. There was only one flight a week to Honiara, so we would have to spend several days in Lata. We felt a bit miserable, standing on the quay on Christmas morning, with no presents for the children and no Christmas dinner to look forward to.

We had forgotten the excellent Solomon Islands

government rest houses. Every town has one of these rest houses, originally intended for government officials there on business. Fortunately, the government rest house in Lata had space for us all. It was Christmas, so no government official was likely to be needing the rooms. So, we had accommodation, not luxurious, not even very clean, but it was somewhere.

We found a small shop that was open and stocked the basics, mostly tinned food, but also flour and cooking oil. So, now we had our Christmas dinner too, albeit rather simple. I made some chapattis, and we ate them with fried luncheon meat and tinned tomatoes. We were hungry and really enjoyed the meal. The disappointment we had felt on the quayside had disappeared and we were able to look forward to this extension of our holiday. We were 'obliged' to spend the next few days wandering around in the sunshine, along beaches of apricot-coloured sand, our children joining in with the locals playing in the surf. It wasn't so tough after all!

A few days later, we managed to get on the flight to Honiara. We were all happy to be back home after our adventures. Our Christmas present to the children was a TV and a video player. They were overjoyed. There was no live television in the Solomons when we were there, except for a temporary service that was set up to cover the Barcelona Olympic Games, a few months before we left. In many ways, we welcomed the lack of TV, as it encouraged the children to look for other activities outside the house. But their friends all had one, and we did not want them to feel left out. I can still remember the first film we rented from the local shop — "Bedknobs and Broomsticks." The children watched it so many times that they could – and did - lie in bed before going to sleep, repeating the entire soundtrack to each other word for word!

About a year later, we went to Q Island, a resort in the western Solomons. This time we went there by ship from Honiara. The ship was a well-known one called the *Yuminao.* (Try saying 'Yu - mi -nao' and guess at its meaning . . .) A neighbour of ours, Ganita, worked on the *Yuminao.* We got to know him and his wife quite well. He was a short, handsome man and his wife was very beautiful, with her hair combed out in an afro, and a ready smile. They had a son of about four, and Ganita's wife was expecting another baby. A month later she gave birth to a baby girl. She gave her the name Aisha, after me. This was because when she went into labour, I drove her to the hospital, and this was her way of saying "thank you." I was very touched and honoured. Ganita was on the ship when we travelled to Q Island. Mani, Farida and Nurudin were happy to see him, they loved Ganita because he was so kind. He bought them snacks and showed them around the ship, even allowing them onto the steering deck, which they found very exciting.

We had a great time on the *Yuminao.* We passed other small Islands, where people on the shoreline waved at us and the ship would hoot back. At some islands we stopped for people to get on or off. Whenever we approached, people in small boats, which were always called canoes in the Solomons, would paddle out to sell us drinks and snacks. Most islands had coconut palms growing on them, and the Solomon Islanders prepared coconut 'milk' from the flesh of mature coconuts, for use in cooking. Coconut water, from the younger coconuts, was a favourite drink but also an important supplement to ordinary water supplies on some islands.

This reminded me of the *Waswahili* of Mombasa, who also cook a lot with coconut milk. It adds a sweet, creamy flavour to the food. My extended family in Kenya cook with coconut milk too. In England I occasionally use coconut cream in a packet bought from a supermarket, but it doesn't quite taste the same as a freshly grated coconut. In Kenya, we obtained the milk by first removing the rough outer skin of a coconut, and then cutting it in half. The hard white flesh lining the inside of the coconut is grated into a bowl using a special grater designed for the purpose. The appearance of this grater is hard to describe, except to say that to use it, you have to sit on it. Its Swahili name is *mbuzi*, or "goat," because that's what it looks like. Once the coconut flesh has been grated into the bowl, a little water is added. We then mix the flesh with (clean) hands for a minute or so before squeezing the mixture through a sieve into another bowl to get the milk out.

People on the Kenyan coast also drink coconut water before the fruit is mature and while the flesh inside the coconut is still tender and slimy. When I was growing up, I was told that it was good for one's health. Apparently, the *Waswahili* believe that men should not drink too much coconut water, however, because they say it can cause the testicles to swell. I have also heard that coconut flesh and water can raise blood cholesterol levels. I guess everything has to be eaten in moderation.

We arrived on Q Island and I must admit, I preferred it to the Reef Islands. It was bigger and more open than the Reef Islands. There were people on the beaches but it was not too crowded, and everyone seemed relaxed. Dolphins could be seen out at sea, which was a great delight for us. We all loved Q Island. The day after we arrived, it was John's birthday. The children decided to go to the beach, which was just a few yards from the chalet we had rented. They wanted to make something special for their dad, so they collected a handful of hermit crabs from the beach and cooked them in seawater in a coconut shell. Singing "Happy Birthday to You", they brought John the hermit crab soup in a coconut shell. John was very grateful but had to decline the soup!

We stayed for a week on Q Island and spent most of the time on the beach, swimming and just relaxing. I collected some nice shells, which I should not really have done. The week flew by, and then it was time to return to Honiara so that John could get back to work. The children were looking forward to seeing Ganita again, but he was not on the ship for the return journey.

MAKIRA ISLAND

Makira is one of the larger islands in the Solomons, south-east of Guadalcanal. Like Guadalcanal, it is an island of mountains and thick forest. I have never been to Makira. So why do I write about it here, under 'Travels'? The answer is that Makira was the home island of our house girl and close friend, Roselyn. Through talking to Roselyn almost every day I learned a lot about her home – probably more than I would have learned by going there. It was a process of 'visiting through conversations' – and that is why I am writing about Makira here.

One day, I asked Roselyn about marriage customs in Makira. She told me that, when a boy has found a girl he likes and has got to know her well enough to decide he would like to marry her, he asks his parents for their approval. They will generally approve of his choice, as long as the girl is not from Malaita Island. Malaitans, she told me, are believed to be quick-tempered and inclined to fight. Once the boy has his parents' approval, the couple ask the girl's parents if they will agree to the marriage. This is different from my own culture because amongst the *Wapare* it is usually the boy's parents who approach the girl's family to break the news, not the couple themselves. The two sets of parents discuss and decide together whether they agree to the marriage. In Makira, Roselyn continued, if the girl's parents approve, then a date would be set for the marriage. The girl is then "tested" by the boy's parents to make sure she is the right girl for their son. The girl is given some tasks, which she must complete in front of a select group of villagers, who assess how hard she works. This "test" takes place at the compound of the boy's parents: her ability to work hard is the measure of her suitability as a wife!

Before the "test," the compound is swept clean, and made ready for the arrival of the girl. The boy sits in his room with the window open, facing the villagers. When the villagers arrive, they sit outside on benches, logs or mats, ready to watch and applaud the girl's performance. A "master of ceremonies" announces the tasks as they take place. The villagers are served with food, such as rice, sweet potatoes, yams, fish and pork, all cooked in coconut milk. They are offered a choice of drinks,. including alcohol, soft drinks or coconut milk, and after their meal they are served with sugar cane and bananas. There is a special reason for this choice of 'sweets' on this occasion. As the guests eat them they throw the sugar cane stalks and banana skins on the floor, and then watch to see how quickly the girl picks them up to keep the compound clean. This is one of the challenges she must meet if she wants to marry the boy! Some of them might throw the rubbish as far as they can, to make it more difficult for the girl, which I think is mean. Meanwhile, the boy has to watch his girl through the window (with his fingers crossed), feeling helpless that he is not allowed to help her.

After an hour, the girl is told to go to the forest and collect a bundle of firewood, while the villagers continue drinking, laughing and joking until she returns. The girl - if she really wants to marry the boy - has to bring as much firewood as she can carry. According to Roselyn, the girl would have been prepared for these tasks of this kind through her upbringing as a girl, so she knows what to expect in the test.

Once the girl has returned from collecting firewood, the boy's parents and the villagers will rate her performance. In almost all cases, Rosalyn said, the villagers will approve her work, and she and the boy can marry, with the ceremony being carried out on that very day..

In my African culture, too, the women have to prove themselves capable of hard work if they want to be accepted for marriage. It is like a competition: if you are lazy, it will be harder for you to get married. In both cultures, the boys do not have to prove themselves, the onus is all on the girl. It's not fair! It seems to be assumed that boys already know everything they need to know for a successful marriage. Perhaps if they were to be tested and approved or disapproved before they could marry, there might be fewer 'problem marriages'.

When I told my mother how marriages are conducted in Makira, she said she would rather stay single and not have to waste her time collecting sugarcane stalks and banana skins just to get married. She could not understand why it should only be the girls who have to show how hard they can work. This was typical of my mother's independent way of thinking. I admired her for that.

CHAPTER 4

MORE TRAVELS

VANUATU

After working two years in Honiara, John was entitled to three months' annual leave. This was later changed to six weeks' holiday a year, which we thought was better. One year, we travelled around the Pacific rather than going back to the UK. We started by flying to Port Vila, the capital of Vanuatu, another group of islands to the south of the Solomon Islands.

Our trip to Vanuatu also gave us an opportunity to visit a couple of our friends from Honiara, Iline and Bill. Iline was originally from the Solomon Islands and Bill was from Australia. They were both very nice and easy to talk to. Iline and I used to take aerobic classes together and became really good friends. Unfortunately, Iline and Bill could not have children, but Bill had a grown-up daughter from a previous marriage, who lived and worked in Sydney.

When Iline and Bill were still living in Honiara, they invited us to their house for lunch one day. Their house was situated on a hill overlooking a beautiful wooded valley, which attracted lots of birds. We arrived at the house and were greeted by two dogs, one of which was wearing a nappy! I asked Iline why the dog was dressed that way, and she told me that the dog was in her period. I had never heard of such a thing. I guess it is not a topic anyone would raise if they were not asked. But I had learnt something and, as they say, it is never too late to learn.

Unfortunately, Tuni, our elder daughter could not join us on our trip to Vanuatu, as she was still at school in New Zealand. John, I, and the rest of the children visited Iline and Bill. It was great to catch up with them again. We had a very nice meal, but could not stay with them because there were so many of us, so we stayed in a hotel not too far from where they lived.

The hotel was beside a river, which had lots of little fish in it. The children were determined to catch some, using a technique Mani had heard about from one of his friends in Honiara. For a rod he used a flexible stick with a length of string for the line, to which he attached a safety pin as a hook and a piece of bread as bait. Much to his surprise, he caught a small fish after dangling the bait in the water for just a short time. He was delighted with his success. It was the very first time he had ever caught a fish. In England he had been told that some fishermen would put maggots under their tongue to warm them before attaching them to the hook, especially on a cold day. Warming them would make them wriggle when they came in contact with the cold water. Mani had been disgusted at this and had never wanted to try fishing. Now he was happy to find that he could still catch a fish without having mouth-warmed maggots, although disappointed when John advised him to put the fish back into the river, or else it would die.

After a few days in Port Vila, we flew to Tana Island to see an active volcano called Yasur. The plane to Tana Island was very small, which meant we had to travel separately, Farida, Nurudin and I on the first flight, and John and Mani on the next one. I was nervous but tried to put a brave face on it in front of the children. I was surprised to see that the pilot wasn't in a separate cabin from the passengers. This made me even more nervous, but being able to see the pilot at work fascinated the children. As for me, I remained calm on the surface but underneath I felt my heart pumping hard.

The entire flight was bumpy, causing the drinks on the little tables to spill. As we descended, the plane was thrown all over the place, until, suddenly the ground rose up to meet us. This airfield was called White Grass Airport. I never did discover why. We landed safely, but as the plane was taxiing to a stop, we saw a couple of dogs beside the airstrip. I discovered later that the dogs were there to chase pigs away whenever a plane was about to land. Apparently, there were pigs in the nearby forest, that often wandered onto the landing strip. The dogs were part of airport security!

A couple of hours later, John and Mani arrived and we compared bumpy flights. They, too, had seen the dogs and wondered what they were doing there. We took a taxi to the hotel, which was very nice, with friendly, welcoming staff and clean rooms. We had a snack in our room, but the children were still peckish, so we took them downstairs to the restaurant. They had sandwiches and drinks while John and I had tea and cassava cake, which I had never tried before. It was very tasty, so I asked someone for the recipe. In case you would like to try it, here are the ingredients that I was given (although I am sorry I can't remember the quantities): grated cassava, plain flour, sugar, desiccated coconut, butter, sodium bicarbonate, eggs and warm water. I tried to cook it once, and it tasted very nice. Why not try experimenting yourself!

The following day, we and a few other tourists took a four-wheel drive vehicle to Mt. Yasur. I had never seen an active volcano close-up before and did not know what to expect. In order to see the hot lava inside the crater better, we set off in the late afternoon, so that it would be quite dark when we got to the top. We were asked before we went what we would like for supper when we returned, which was expected to be at about nine or ten o'clock.

The road to the volcano was narrow and the surface poor, but this was all part of the excitement. After about two hours, we arrived at the bottom of Mt Yasur. Here, a complication arose. We should have climbed up from that point and come back down to the same point to be picked up. The trouble was, the collection point was right on the edge of a lake. It had been raining a lot, and still was, so the water level was rising. The driver told us he could not be sure of getting back to this point before the water covered the road. He said that while we were climbing up he would dash back past the edge of the lake and meet us on the other side of the volcano. This meant we had to go up to the edge of the crater as planned, then walk around the edge before we came down. The driver stopped and dropped everyone and he advised us which way to go up the mountain and which side to come down. The driver said he would be waiting for us at the agreed place and the time.

We got off the bus and started to climb. We were the only people with children, so we took the easiest route. It took us quite a while to reach the crater. As we climbed, we could hear the volcano thundering away beneath us. It would be truer to say that we felt it through our bodies more than just hearing it! We reached the top and looked down into the crater. Gases were swirling around above the lava bubbling below us with a red-hot glow. I was getting a bit worried as usual. Seeing all that hot lava being forced up made me very anxious. Would it burst out on top of us? Supposing one of the children fell in, they would be cooked in seconds! The best thing was not to think about it too much or show my concerns, otherwise I would spoil the excitement. But I was very careful.

The children were fascinated but I was still worried, and we could see mist beginning to come down, so we decided it was time to go. Now we were really in trouble. We couldn't go back the way we had come, so where was the way down? Darkness was rapidly falling and the mist was growing thicker. There was a strong smell of sulphur in the air. All we could do was scramble down over the ash and loose stones. In the end we decided to sit and just slide down. I was terrified, sure we were all going to meet our end on this dark mountain, and no one would find us. I am not all that brave, and I always worry about the children. Needless to say, they found it very exciting.

It was almost midnight when we reached the bottom of the mountain and we were left with torn clothes because of sliding down on the coarse ash and loose stones. We met up with the others, who were worried about us. We said we were sorry for delaying everyone like this, and explained that we'd lost our way. No one seemed to notice our torn clothes and almost bare backsides.

We were tired and hungry, and the journey back to our hotel felt very long. We finally arrived at three in the morning and were met by two people waiting for us at the hotel reception. We went to our rooms, showered, changed and went back downstairs, where we were served with the evening meal we had ordered before setting off, expecting to be back five or six hours earlier than we were! We were so hungry that we enjoyed that meal even more than we would have done if we had been on time! I was told by the hotel manager that I was the first African to have climbed Mt Yasur. That was nice to know! As much as I was scared for my family, I am glad to have had that opportunity of climbing a live volcano, something I had never dreamed of doing.

After a few days on Tana Island, we flew back to Port Vila and then on to Noumea, the capital of New Caledonia, which is still administered by the French. We only stayed there for one day and all I remember of Noumea is walking along the beach and seeing a half-naked woman sunbathing. I commented to John in *Kiswahili,* "Kuna *nyama* nyingi" meaning "there is a lot of flesh." She came up to us a bit later and asked, "Was that the *Kiswahili* you were speaking?" We were really embarrassed until it turned out she hadn't understood what I was saying. She told us she had lived in Dar-es-Salaam for a while, and had picked up a bit of *Kiswahili*. The encounter taught me not to make rude comments in *Kiswahili* – or any other language —you never knew who might have understood!

New Zealand

From Noumea we flew to Auckland in New Zealand to pick up Tuni. We wanted to see more of this beautiful country than we had last time we visited, when we had been so captivated by just the northern part of North Island and its friendly inhabitants, that we didn't get round to exploring any further. So this time we hired a car and set off with the intention of driving around the southern part of North Island before crossing to South Island. Once again, however, North Island worked its magic on us and we never did get to see South Island. As we drove, we realised we did not want to rush around and in the end, decided it was a better idea to take time just to enjoy the bits we passed through. South Island, we thought, would always be there 'next time'. We travelled around the Coromandel Peninsula and stayed a night there even though we had originally thought we could just 'pass through'. It was just so beautiful that we had to linger and enjoy it, stopping at beaches along the way.

The furthest we actually got was Rotorua, where we arrived just before Christmas. We decided it would be a great place to spend Christmas Day. I was fascinated by the volcanic landscape. We soon got used to the smell of sulphur from the hot springs and mud pools that seemed to appear everywhere, and it didn't spoil our enjoyment at all. Because it was Christmas we made a special trip up into the nearby mountains in the hope of finding snow – and we did! We have a picture of Tuni holding up a snowball she had made on Christmas Eve, but looking very cold indeed. It was summer in New Zealand but the cold gave it a Christmassy feel for us. All we lacked was a Christmas tree, so, when no one was looking, we carefully cut a small 'Christmas twig' from one of the pine trees and stuck it in a bottle. Our Christmas dinner was not the traditional English meal but one that our children always enjoy: chapattis and kidney beans cooked in coconut cream, with fresh tomatoes, onions, and curry powder. To this day this is the meal the children hope we will prepare for them at least once when they come to visit us. We even had Christmas presents for the children. They had seen us buying these in Auckland, so we told them that this year we were doing Santa's job for him since he wouldn't be able to find us so far from home.

WESTERN SAMOA

The following day – which should have been Boxing Day - we flew to Western Samoa in time to have a second Christmas Day. Though they are near each other, there is a twenty-four-hour time difference between New Zealand and Samoa because they are on opposite sides of the international dateline, and that is why we had two Christmas Days in one year. On the evening of our second Christmas Day we were entertained by the hotel staff in the famous Aggie Grey's Hotel with an impressive performance of Samoan singing and dancing.

We spent Christmas and Boxing Day in the capital, Apia, and then went to stay with the family of my friend Tino. They lived on another of the Western Samoan islands, so we had to take a ferry to get there. While we waited for Tino's brother to pick us up on the other side of the ferry, the children got a bit restless, just hanging around. There was nothing much there other than a couple of small shops selling drinks and things for waiting travellers. Unfortunately, before Tino's brother arrived, Nurudin got bitten on the leg by a scruffy-looking stray dog that had been wandering around looking for scraps of food. Even though it didn't seem to be a serious bite we were worried about it, knowing that there is rabies in the Pacific islands and we had no idea what medical facilities were nearby; so we kept a close eye on him for the next few days. Fortunately, he was OK.

Tino's family lived in a pretty village of traditional Samoan houses surrounded by palm trees, which provided welcome shade but still allowed flickering sunshine and views of a clear blue sky. Tino's family welcomed us with big smiles and fed us very generously. A teenage relative and some of her friends took us for a walk around the village. We met other groups, all out for an afternoon stroll and chats with friends. Everyone seemed so relaxed. Being unusual visitors to the village we attracted a lot of attention and many stopped to ask about us, where we were from, who we were visiting and so on. This was all done in such a welcoming, friendly way, with lots of smiles and giggles. One group of teenage girls had particularly good English and it turned out they were at school in neighbouring American Samoa. They boarded there and came back to the village during school holidays. They were particularly excited to see us. Our lasting impressions of the few days we spent in the village are of warmth and colour - the people, the clothes they wore, the sunshine and flowers everywhere.

Tino's family house was built in Samoan traditional style, referred to as a "fale" (pronounced "far-lay"). My first impression of this fale was that it had no walls. On closer inspection, I saw that the walls had been folded up! When it began to get dark, the walls were unfolded so that they hung downwards. They were made from dried palm-leaves woven together like some kind of basket-work. This makes them light and easy to fold, while still being windproof. The floors were also covered with woven mats which people sit or lie on, whether relaxing, napping or just sitting and talking to family and neighbours. In a hot, humid climate like that of Samoa this makes a great deal of sense, you don't need solid walls to keep out the cold. In the daytime, the absence of walls allows the breeze through the house, keeping it cooler, although it also means that passers-by can see in. In the evening, the unfolded walls give privacy, as well as keeping out mosquitoes and other night-flying insects. As in Africa, some concessions to modernity have been made. Corrugated iron roofs, for example, have replaced the traditional thatch, though they have retained their distinctive "Samoan" appearance. The houses are beautiful while also allowing for the particular conditions in Samoa. I had never seen any houses quite like them, and I was impressed by the good sense behind their design.

The way Samoan men dress reminded me of the *Waswahili* of Mombasa. They usually wear a T-shirt and a lava-lava, a sarong made of colourful material wrapped around their waists and reaching down to their knees; much cooler than trousers. The East African equivalent to the lava-lava is the *lesso, kitenge,* or *shuka* worn by women, or the *kikoi* for men. The *lesso* is used for all sorts of purposes, not just to wear. We use a *lesso* to strap our babies on our backs, as a mat to sit on, as a headscarf, and much, much more. Even here in England, John and I often wear one around the house if it is warm. For one thing, it is easier to put on than all those European clothes! For some reason John and I tend to use the Samoan name, lava-lava, for this garment, rather than any of the Swahili terms.

Like the Solomon Islanders, Samoan people place garlands of flowers around the necks of arriving and departing visitors. These garlands, called leis, are worn whenever there is a special occasion, but we came across them most often as a token of greeting or farewell. When we finally departed from the Solomon Islands, so many friends came to see us off at Honiara airport, and we all ceremoniously had leis placed around our neck. In the Solomon Islands, the flower most often used for making a lei is the frangipani, so arrivals and departures were accompanied by an atmosphere full of the sweet, delicate scent of these flowers. Whenever I smell frangipani now, I am transported back to our time in various Pacific islands.

Aspects of Samoan culture remind me of my own African culture, particularly in that family is extremely important to them. There are also similarities in much of the food they grow and eat. Samoans grow many of the crops we grow in Africa, such as sweet potatoes, cassava, yams, bananas, and coconut palms; vegetables such as okra, cabbage, spinach, spring cabbage and kidney beans. They eat a lot of fresh fish and pork and cook with coconut cream or desiccated coconut like the Solomon Islanders. Delicious! One food popular in Samoa and much of the rest of the Pacific, but which I never came across – let alone ate – in East Africa is shellfish. Once, Tino and I were swimming at Bonegi beach and she picked up a live clam from the seabed. Informing me, "This is how we eat them," she split the shell open and popped the contents into her mouth, chewed it and swallowed it. I was horrified! I certainly could not have done it. Even now, the thought of it makes me wince. But she enjoyed it and went looking for more!

The Samoans tend to be big-boned athletic people, with light skin and dark silky hair. Many Samoan men have their backs, arms, legs and neck covered in tattoos. Tino's younger brother was a traditional tattooist and while we were there, John decided to ask him for a tattoo. It would make an excellent souvenir and a permanent reminder of our stay in Samoa. He thought a traditional Samoan, whole-body tattoo would be a bit much, so he settled for just a leopard on his upper arm, but tattooed using the traditional Samoan way. I watched it being done. Tino's brother used a sharp needle, and it looked very painful, though John said it hardly hurt at all.

I have to admit that I dislike tattoos. In Britain, I once saw a man with half his face covered with a tattoo depicting a spider's web. It made me uncomfortable just to look at him. Perhaps there is a cultural element to my reaction since the *Wapare* do not practice tattooing. However, John's leopard tattoo has not led to divorce!

JORDAN

When we retired, John and I decided that we wanted to continue travelling to new places while we could still manage it and could afford to. We are very fortunate that our daughter, Farida, and her family live in Dubai. Going to visit them offers us the opportunity to piggyback on such visits and see places closer to Dubai than England. One year, having spent two weeks in Dubai, we decided to go to Petra, in Jordan. Being older than we were in our globe-trotting days, we wanted an 'easier' holiday in which all arrangements were made for us in advance by a travel agent. So, through an agency, we booked not only our flight to Amman, the capital of Jordan, but also got them to arrange all the subsequent travel itinerary and details, rather than making it up as we went along, as we used to do.

The flight to Amman was rather bumpy at times, and, as always, I was nervous. We were met at the airport by our driver, who was very welcoming and friendly, and put me at ease again after the flight. He greeted us with a handshake and a big smile as he said, '"Welcome to Amman!" He was to be our driver for our entire stay, and from the very start he did everything he could to put us at our ease. He helped us with our luggage and opened the car door for us as I would expect a gentleman to do! He had provided bottled water for the journey to our hotel at Wadi Musa, next to Petra but 140 miles from Amman. The long drive to Wadi Musa gave us plenty of time to get to know one another. Our driver, Muhammed, told us about his life and that he was still a single man, despite his age, which I guessed to be about forty. He said he was still looking for a partner, but he could not afford to pay a dowry, which reminded me again of my own culture. He lived with his parents or stayed with friends.

The landscape was arid, with the occasional shrub and dwelling. As evening approached and the light was fading, Muhammed took a short diversion, in order to show us a ruined Crusader castle, which looked really dramatic against the sinking sun. A few hours into our journey, we stopped at a big roadside shop, which was clearly aimed at tourists because they had items on sale that were obviously far too expensive for ordinary people — including us! The shopkeepers offered John and I a cup of tea which we drank at a small table, while Muhammed sat apart, chatting in Arabic with a group of other men. We browsed the goods on sale without any real intention of buying anything, before going to pay for our tea, which the shopkeeper told us was free. He tried to tempt us into buying something, pointing out particular 'treasures' he thought we might like. "Maybe next time," we said, though I have to admit we were tempted by some of the amazing items on show, but quite apart from the cost, which in some cases ran into hundreds of pounds, we simply would not have been able to carry them because of their size. Or maybe that just gave us a convenient means of escape from paying out sums of money we would later have regretted, although the shopkeeper insisted he could always arrange for shipment. So, we were grateful for the tea but happy to leave with a smile and a 'Maybe next time!'

So we continued our journey. There was little to see in the desert landscape apart from the odd tree. I think these were olives, which at least softened the harsh landscape, adding touches of green to the miles of rock and sand. We didn't see any birds or animals, except for a few camels occasionally. At last, we arrived at our hotel, a modern building situated on a small hill overlooking a few scattered dwellings. The people at the hotel were very friendly and welcoming and greeted us with a smile. A young man helped us with our suitcases and took us to our room, which may seem unremarkable, except that in our travels we had often been in hotels where we were given the key and directions to the lift! Our room was large with a view across the desert to some shrubs that indicated the town of Wadi Musa, from which visitors gain access to Petra. After putting our suitcases away, we went to see Muhammed, who was waiting for us at the reception, to make arrangements for the following day. He told us he would come back the next morning to collect us. John and I had yet another cup of tea (of course!) and strolled around the hotel grounds, where we took some photos of the setting sun highlighting the ridges surrounding the town. The hotel didn't appear to have many guests, which was understandable, as there was nothing much to see.

I have to admit that I knew next to nothing about Petra and what to expect there. I don't think John knew very much either, but like many people, he had seen images of it in the film "Indiana Jones and the Last Crusade." In fact, the film was what had prompted him to suggest this journey to me, and it turned out we were not alone in that. Just outside the official entrance to the Petra site, we noticed the "Indiana Jones Gift Shop." This made us laugh, but our guide, who had taken over from Mohammed for our visit to the Petra site itself, pointed out that the film had greatly benefited the local economy. It had triggered a huge increase in tourism to Petra and that led him to switch, for part of the year at least, from being the engineer that he had trained to be, first to study all about the site and then qualify as a tour guide. This, he said, paid more than engineering and it was a more reliable job.

To get access to the main part of the city of Petra, one must walk through a winding, deep and narrow gorge called the "*Siq*," also to be seen in the Indiana Jones film. We found this gorge to be even more impressive than the film suggests. As we walked further in, the vertical sides of the gorge became higher and higher, narrower and narrower until only glimpses of the blue sky could be seen above us, making us feel small and insignificant in the face of nature. But the *Siq* is more than just a deep gash in the earth's surface. It has a human history too, and we were glad of a guide who could point out different features and explain their history and significance. It was completely different from anything I had ever seen, with its tombs and stones worn into strange shapes by nature or carved by human beings. Some rocks were naturally streaked with colours from pale yellows to rose-reds, while others had been carved to represent lions.

As we continued to follow the gorge, eventually we

arrived at the narrowest, darkest part but through the narrow gap ahead of us, like a strip of light, we saw something wonderful. We glimpsed stone columns and the façade of a magnificent building - but only a glimpse. As we drew closer, the gap widened and we saw... Wow! Carved into the rock, was the "Treasury", though to us it looked more like a temple, with a large doorway and columns supporting a decorated triangular roof. When we emerged from the *Siq*, we could see it wasn't a separate building, but had been carved into the rock. It takes a while to realise this. We had seen it in the film, but seeing it for real was something else. It took our breath away. Despite its name, it is actually an enormous tomb, so visitors are not allowed to go inside. I don't know if this is out of respect for the people buried there, or to prevent tourists from damaging this amazing 2000-year-old treasure.

Our first sight of the whole building was so compelling that it was a while before we realised that the open space in front of the Treasury was busy with small restaurants, stalls selling souvenirs, people making tea in whatever free space they could find, camels and pony-carts offering to carry visitors further into Petra, and of course, people taking photos of the Treasury from every angle. We were surrounded by tall red crags, dry and bare. It all felt very otherworldly; walking down that long narrow *Siq* and suddenly coming upon this magnificent edifice added to the sense of mystery. We were approached by a young man who pointed out a rocky ledge, high up and facing the Treasury. He asked us if we would like to take tea up there. We were easily persuaded! He led the way up what was quite a climb to a ledge covered in coloured woven rugs. Here, an older man was tending a small stove beside some large flasks of tea. Sitting on the rugs, John and I drank our tea admiring a grandstand view of the Treasury and all the activity below us. From our vantage point we watched people with camels and pony-carriages trying to persuade tourists that it really is a long hot walk into the site and a camel or a carriage would be much more comfortable: so please take a ride. After taking the first part on foot, we too switched to a pair of donkeys. It was the first time I'd ever ridden a donkey and I found it uncomfortable. I am glad I tried but I don't think I'll be doing it again.

What fascinated me was how the steep natural rock sides of the valley had been made to look like terraced houses. These "houses" were carved into the rock face, a façade with open windows and doors into the rock. Some looked especially grand and ornate, and we were told these were the Royal Tombs, because they are carved intricately than the others. Other rock faces were plainer, with wide, deep holes into the rock. These, we were told, were the tombs for ordinary people. Others had once had people living in them, who had made wooden extensions in front of them that have disappeared over the years. We did not have to be very close to see every detail carved into these rocks; they were huge and impressive even at a distance. Another hillside had been carved into a theatre that could hold an audience of 4000! The seats were like rows of steps carved into a great curved rock face, in front of which was the stage.

There was more to see than what I have described: the ruins of a great temple, for example, and rows of stone columns which marked where a street had once been. We could have stayed longer and walked further, but we were getting very hot, thirsty and tired. I really would encourage you to go and see it for yourself; it is an amazing sight and an unforgettable experience.

After spending several hours in the city ruins, we went back to find our driver, Mohammed. It was a long way to walk, so we walked as far as we could and then took a horse ride — not a donkey this time — back to the site entrance, where Mohammed was waiting for us. Riding the horse was more comfortable than the donkey, although I could never have ridden it without someone leading me. I would happily do it again if I had another opportunity.

That afternoon, Mohammed drove us further south, into the desert, to a place called Wadi Rum. It was quite a long journey and the land grew drier and drier, until it was nothing but sand and huge, red rocky outcrops. In the middle of these we found camps for tourists consisting of chalets or fancy tents. We were shown to our chalet, which was simple but comfortable. At this point, Mohammed left us to explore the desert by ourselves. I had never been to a desert, so this was another new experience for me. Before me stretched endless miles of desert, as far as the eye could see. It was very beautiful, especially in the evening and early morning when the sun was just above the horizon, with bands of orange cloud in the sky. The morning and evening breeze was very welcome, because it became very hot in the middle of the day.

John and I decided to explore the desert. We had a choice of horse, camel or 4x4 vehicle. We decided to forego the pleasure of any more horse or camel rides and arranged for one of the 4x4s to take us, as Mohammed was resting after his long drive. Our driver was young and rather grumpy, but we were there during Ramadan, so he was fasting. He drove a bit too fast for our comfort, and I asked him to slow down. It was really bumpy, and not much fun. The young driver looked sullen, and I wondered whether this was because he resented being told what to do by a woman, especially by a black woman! I felt that maybe I should know my place!

Anyway, he did slow down a bit, although sometimes he could not avoid throwing us around in our seats when we had to go through very thick sand. He drove us to a certain point, where he said we could get out and walk around to see the scenery better. The scenery was rocks and sand, which may not sound very interesting but it was dramatic and new to me, so I didn't complain. The key to enjoyable travel, I have found, is to appreciate places for what they are, to look for the beauty and interest in them rather than comparing them with other places. And certainly, as the sun set, this shining red desert scenery was genuinely lovely.

There were several groups of tourists arriving on camels or horses and others in cars, like us. A large shop had even been set up there in the middle of nowhere, where we bought souvenirs and perfumes (some of which I am still using). Then I discovered why tourists came to this particular spot. Many of you will know of Lawrence of Arabia — even if only through the film — but the name meant nothing to me. Now learned something about the history of this part of the world, and the role T.E. Lawrence played in it. A rock, carved with his face on it, bore an inscription explaining that it was in this place that Lawrence met up with the local Arab leaders and helped them begin their fight for independence from the Ottoman Empire. If you have seen the film, you will know about it; if you haven't, then do look for it as it is a great film.

After our exploration of the rocks and sand, it was time to go back so the driver could break his fast. He drove us back to our chalet, where we showered and changed, and then went to the restaurant for a buffet supper. The food was so tasty we kept going back for more. The desert doesn't just make you thirsty, it gives you an appetite! We even had some lovely local desert desserts!

After our Wadi Rum excursion, we headed back through the desert to Amman. The wide expanse of dry landscape dotted with shrubs and occasional buildings, under a cloudless blue sky was beautiful in its way, but I would not like to live there; it was just too dry for me.

Near Amman we were taken to the city of Madaba to see an old Christian church. On the floor of this church are the remains of a sixth-century mosaic showing a map of the Holy Land. The original church was destroyed in an earthquake and the mosaic was damaged, so it is no longer complete, but it is still very interesting. It is the oldest known map of this part of the world, and a guide pointed out different places mentioned in the Bible, such as Jerusalem, and the Dead Sea, along with other places that no longer exist. Apparently, archaeologists have excavated these places and found their remains, showing how skilled the map-makers were, even then, all those centuries ago.

From Madaba we were driven up to the top of a high ridge known as Mount Nebo. I don't know about you, but

I had never heard of Mount Nebo before. When I learned what it is famous for, I felt quite strange — honoured too — because I found that I was standing where Moses is supposed to have stood thousands of years ago. The Old Testament says that Moses led the Jewish people out of Egypt, where they had been slaves. They wandered in the desert for forty years, looking for the land that God had promised them. After forty years had passed, God led Moses alone up to a mountain top from where he could see the Promised Land. Moses himself was never to enter it, as he had once broken God's Faith. That mountain top was Mount Nebo. And there I was, looking across to the "Promised Land." Can you understand why I felt honoured? I had never dreamt that I would stand on this mountain where Moses supposedly stood when God spoke to him. I could almost feel myself in Moses's skin; maybe God would give me the instructions to enter his Promised Land. It was like a dream waiting to happen.

I expect most of you know all about the Dead Sea, why it is called "Dead," and the strange properties it has. Not me. I had heard the name when I was in primary school, but I never thought about it - why it was 'dead', for example. It was just a name to me, and I assumed it was just a sea, like the seas I was familiar with, where you can swim and snorkel and splash about. In fact, my experience when I got to the Dead Sea just amazed me. Now I know what the "Dead" really means!

We arrived at the Dead Sea Resort, checked in and were shown our room, which looked out over several swimming pools where attendants were keeping an eye on the swimmers to make sure they were safe. It all looked very organised, a nice place to come for a holiday — but not to live in. The surrounding landscape was again rather too dry and barren for me. I have always associated dry, barren landscapes with hard times, probably because of my farming background. The hotel gardens had been planted with bougainvillaea and other drought-resistant shrubs, which made the surroundings greener and really colourful, but they could not hide the distant dry hills. The paths had been made to look like a maze, where you never know what is round the next corner, which was usually another swimming pool!

We decided to go down to the edge of Dead Sea, about ten minutes' walk away, but not to swim just yet. It was already getting late, and we were tired and hot. From a distance, we could see people in the water, but I assumed they were just enjoying a swim in the sea, as people do at the seaside. But it was getting too hot to walk any closer, so we sat in the shade of a large umbrella and gazed out at the blue sea against the blue sky, with a distant view of the opposite shore, in Israel.

The next day, after our breakfast, I was looking forward to having a swim, since the last time I had done so was when we were living in the Solomon Islands. The seas around Britain are just too cold for me! We arrived at the beach and I stopped in amazement. None of the people in the sea were actually swimming. They were all floating on their backs with their heads and most of their bodies above the water. They looked as though they were just sitting back in an armchair. Some of them were giggling. They seemed to be trying to stand and finding it difficult. It was almost as if they were drunk! John and I joined the crowd and ventured into the water. I found myself behaving just like everyone else, lying back and rocking in the sea — and I was definitely not drunk! I felt weird, but at the same time I enjoyed floating on my back with the feeling of assurance that I won't drown. I had never been really confident in deep water, but now I was able just to relax and enjoy it. The water itself felt different, thicker than ordinary seawater. Of course this was because there is so much salt in it, and I had to be careful not to get it into my eyes, or my mouth. When I tried to stand up, I kept losing my balance and John had to help me. I think I must have looked drunk! There was a lifeguard nearby keeping an eye on the swimmers in case there was a problem — he had to help John stand up! It is difficult to explain just how strange it felt, especially because I had expected it to be just like going into an ordinary sea, but it was fun.

On the beach there were buckets full of what looked like black mud, and people were smearing it all over their bodies and faces. John and I decided to give it a try and covered ourselves with what turned out really to be black mud. It was very smooth, with an almost oily texture. We rubbed it on our bodies and faces and I became even blacker than I am already! One of the lifeguards took a photo of us, all covered in mud. We were told that it was good for the skin. I don't know if it really was but at least it gave John a change from the endless smearing of sun-block. And now I know what 'Dead' Sea means.

Chapter 5

A Tale of Two Villages

I now live in an English village. I grew up in African villages. In that sense, my life has come round in a circle. Reaching the end of my story so far, this might then be a good place for me to look back and reflect on my beginnings and my present – I won't say 'my end'! I want to look at the similarities and differences between village life in Africa and England.

Until I reached my teenage years I lived with my family in three different villages at different times. These were small villages set amongst hills and valleys. As I child, I did not appreciate the landscape. All I knew was that the hills were hard work for my short child's legs. In these villages, life was mostly work. There was little time to be a child. Instead of playing, we were taught from an early age to help with the work in the house and the farm. But I also found there was no time to be a teenager, a time when I might have gone to visit friends for a chat, because there was always work waiting to be done, and that was our life.

Occasionally in the evening during a full moon, we would practise our traditional dancing and singing. Those were happy occasions that have stayed in my memory all these years. They were a welcome break from the routine of daily work.

When I was a teenager, I vowed to myself never to live in a village when I grew up. To me, village life meant work - hard, physical work. I now realise, however, that my village experiences taught me a lot and contributed to who and what I am today. I am glad of the lessons I learned. We were taught to respect our elders, and never to call them by their first names, or answer back, even if they were in the wrong. We were also taught the proper way to shake hands when greeting visitors — always use the right hand and never the left. The left hand is the one you use to wipe your behind.

John and I are now living in the village of Brassington in Derbyshire, between Matlock and Ashbourne. I don't think I could have accepted returning to African village life, because of the experiences I had all those years ago. I wanted to leave all that behind. Somehow, however, I seem to have been convinced that I can enjoy living in a village once more. Now, living in an English village, I cannot believe that I ever wanted to live anywhere else.

My experience of living here has revealed many differences between life in an English village and life in African villages. For a start, they just look different! The houses in Eldoro and Usangi are a mix of thatched and corrugated iron roofs, with walls of either mud or cement blocks. In Brassington, the houses are all made of (or faced with) Derbyshire stone, and have tiled roofs. They are all grey, and must, by the conservation area rules, remain that way. But it is not just the appearance and structure of the houses that differ. They are arranged differently, too. In Usangi, houses are built where the owners have their land, on their farms, and are quite scattered. In Eldoro, land that is good for farming is near the river and is not a good place to build a house, so people tend to live on the higher, drier ground. The houses are therefore grouped closer to each other than in Usangi, though still much further apart than in this English village. The African villages are made up of family compounds, usually with more than one house (all single-story of course) and separate places for keeping the cattle and goats. You never see rows of houses joined together in a terrace, or even semi-detached houses. An African family house stands on its own.

I was going to say that English villages are organised around tarmac roads, whereas African villages are not shaped by any road pattern. But in the case of Brassington (and part of its charm), the houses appear — at first sight anyway — to be arranged in a higgledy-piggledy fashion. Most roads within the village look as though they have been fitted around and between the houses, rather than the other way round. It can be quite difficult for visitors arriving by car, and as for finding somewhere to park — well, that is another story. In our first few days here we went on short walks to explore the village, and sometimes got a bit lost on the way back.

I have been told that all English villages 'must' have two establishments vital to the life of the place: a church and a pub. Well, we do have an attractive old church in Brassington, situated near the top of one side of the valley in which the village stands. From most directions approaching the village, this valley encloses the village making it almost hidden and a bit of a surprise when you come to it. There are only two places from which the whole village can be seen. There's a brief, distant view from the road if you drive in from the Ashbourne direction. To get the other view, you have to climb up the steep opposite side of the valley, but it is worth the effort. Even though we have climbed up there many times, we still pause every time and look back to admire our new home. When you look at the village from a distance, it seems to be spread out around the church, spilling down the hillside. The small track behind the church offers a fascinating view across the village and to the other side of the valley and the hills beyond. It is another place where we cannot resist pausing to take in the view whenever we go for a stroll around the village. It is a great place from which to see the almost chaotic way in which the houses seem to be arranged, as if they really had been accidentally spilled down the hillside.

As for pubs, we still have two in the village, but a map from over a century ago shows that there used to be at least four of five. The two that remain are welcoming places with lovely owners who always seem happy to see us. In the years before we arrived, the village gradually lost its shops and its post office, which one of my friends used to manage. This loss of services in the village has mostly happened within living memory and it would have been easy for the village to lose its community identity and spirit when this happened, but we do get a strong sense that the village remains a community whenever we go for a walk around. As one of our neighbours once said, "You can walk round the village in fifteen minutes, unless you meet people along the way, when it can take as long as you want." We have discovered the truth of this: meeting village people and stopping to chat, exchange news, stroke the dog, and just connect with each other has become part of daily village life.

There are also organised activities, and people in the village go to great lengths to make sure they carry on for the benefit of future generations of villagers. There are quiz nights and Bingo at the pub or British Legion hall, there's an annual fell run, which attracts runners from miles around. We saw this for the first time shortly after we arrived. There were "serious" runners (young and middle-aged), who were really impressive, as well as people who were just joining in for the fun of it. We oldies turned out to support them as they passed. Once a year, we even have a carnival, with a procession of floats and a Carnival Queen (and her little dog).

The church (14th century with later repairs and alterations, not all very well done) is a centre for numerous events, especially at Christmas, when we buy locally made cards and decorations, and at Easter. We are made welcome, even though we are not Christians. There is also bell-ringing, which I am told is a pastime that has many English enthusiasts. It was only when I came to England that I discovered just how much bell-ringing goes on here. When we lived in the Solomon Islands we had a friend who was crazy (in the nicest possible way) about bell-ringing. Although there were no bells for him to ring in the Solomons, he looked for opportunities wherever he travelled, even if it meant going a long way off his intended route. I found this passion for bell-ringing rather strange. In Eldoro there was a single bell that was tolled on Sunday morning to call people to church. In Brassington we have a proper peal of bells (I am told that is the right name for it), and even have a church clock, maintained by a couple of skilled villagers, that rings the hour and all the quarter hours.

I have to admit that our village population of just over 500 contains rather a lot of older people — including myself and John — but we do try to be active and keep the community alive. Perhaps, being older and retired, we have more time on our hands, even if we don't have as much energy as the younger generation.

I often find myself reflecting on the way my life has taken me from living in small African villages when I was young to living in a small village in England now I am older. I have tried here to show some of the differences between these villages, but there are also similarities. In both places, the villages are small, making it easier for the inhabitants to get to know one another and share a sense of community. This was missing in the towns and cities in various countries that we have lived in. Of course, this isn't always the case, because there were Eldoro inhabitants that I did not know very well, just as here in Brassington I cannot claim to know everyone. Eldoro was much more spread out, however, and people were more dispersed, with several different tribes and languages, so the sense of being part of a single village community was perhaps weaker than what we feel here in England. In Eldoro there were other factors influencing who we felt close to, such as family, religion, tribe and language.

One of the biggest differences is that in the African villages, almost everyone was — and indeed still is — a farmer. This was so in Brassington too, in the past. Everyone here was linked to agriculture in some way, either as a farm owner or a farm worker, with a few providing services for the farms, such as a blacksmith. It is interesting seeing evidence for this when we walk around the village. Converted barns are easy to spot and the outlines of earlier doors, windows and even walls are easily identifiable in stone houses such as ours. There are also cottages here that have "Farm" or "Barn" in their name, as well as "Post Office" and "Co-op." There were no traces of history to be seen in the structures or family compounds in Eldoro, and no interest in preserving village history. We looked to the future, especially we younger inhabitants, not the past.

One of the delightful features of Brassington is that the houses have no numbers, only names. This must be a bit of a challenge to the postman! In my African villages, houses were not identifiable by number or name, but then there was no postal delivery service there either. You had to collect the post — such as it was — yourself from the main post office in the nearest town. If you were visiting someone in the village, you weren't given an address; you simply asked anyone you met if they knew where "so-and-so" lived.

Nowadays there are very few farmworkers in Brassington. Where I grew up, we had no choice, because our farms were where we got most of our food.

Nevertheless, I did not enjoy farm work. Like Eldoro, Brassington is surrounded by farmland, but few here depend directly on farming for their living. The farmland around us is used almost entirely for grazing sheep and cows. The Eldoro livestock mostly consisted of goats and sheep, with some cows. We do have a few goats in Brassington. I am writing this after returning from a walk (during a break in the rain), and a friendly miniature goat came across its field to make friends with John. The green hills around us are studded with rocky outcrops and divided up by Derbyshire dry stone walls. Our views are defined by the sides of the valley in which the village lies. They are very attractive views and when the weather is right we indulge ourselves by sitting outside with a mug of tea and warm *mandazi* while we absorb the view, which was one of the reasons we chose this spot. But if we want a grander view to a distant horizon, we have to do a bit of hill climbing first.

In contrast, the landscape in Eldoro was spread out for miles right in front of us when we looked eastwards across the Tsavo plains, and then fell away gently behind us before dramatically sweeping up to the Ugweno Mountains in the west or to magnificent Kilimanjaro towards the north. It was a "big" view, a broad, impressive landscape, dry and even rather barren at times but lush and green after the rains. I never took much time to admire the view in Eldoro; it was just where I lived and I was used to it. No one talked about the view. Nor did I travel in those days, so I had little to compare it with.

Although I am glad that I am no longer obliged to work on the farm, I have developed a love of gardening. I think this is at least partly because tending a garden is a choice, but working on the farm was not. Planting and tending flowers and shrubs simply for their beauty and not just for food is a completely new activity for me, but it seems that although this African has been taken out of the farm, the farm has not been completely taken out of this African. I am delighted that we have inherited fruit trees and gooseberry bushes and even rhubarb from the previous owners, but I have also opened up new plots for different kinds of vegetables that we harvest and eat. And I enjoy doing it. I am not alone in my passion for gardening either. There are some beautiful gardens in Brassington that could only have been made through love, imagination and hard work. There are also allotments in the village where people grow vegetables. Every time we pass them by, I wonder whether I should try to get my own patch of land down there and start some serious "farming." Maybe my memories of the hard work on the land in Kenya are fading!

Less than a week after our arrival in Brassington, we heard a knock at the door and opened it to find a lady holding a bunch of flowers and a bottle of wine. My immediate reaction was that this lady was coming to visit the people who were here before us, and she had not realised that we were the new owners! But she greeted us, introduced herself as Deborah and told us she lived two doors away. She gave us the flowers and wine and said with a smile, "Welcome to our village." We were not expecting this at all, and were touched to receive such a welcome from a total stranger. We had a friendly chat together over an inevitable cup of tea and she told us about the village and some of its characters, giving us a very promising impression of the village. After Deborah left, John and I said to each other, "Wow! What a lovely lady Deborah is." Nowadays, we don't see her as often as we would like to because she works, but whenever we do see her, there is always that friendly smile and a little chat. That was a marvellous introduction to Brassington, which set us up with positive, optimistic expectations of what this new phase in our life could become.

Being welcomed like this was a new experience for me. It would be very unusual in the African villages I grew up in for a stranger to come to your house, introduce themself and bring you a present. People needed to know something about you first before they became familiar. On the other hand, people got to know each other quite quickly because we all shared the same patterns of life. We would make contact with newcomers through the common daily tasks, such as collecting water from the river or firewood from the forest. These activities presented opportunities to talk and share information among ourselves. As we got to know each other, then perhaps invitations to visit us at home would be extended to those with whom we felt some sort of closeness or connection. This is not to say we were unfriendly or uncaring. In times of hardship, such as illness, or a death, the village people would show great kindness and support for each other.

We hadn't lived long in Brassington before we discovered that this sense of community and mutual support was also to be found here. Some of this comes about through meeting people when we are out walking. Dogs, giving people a reason to get out, have often been important in making these encounters happen. Also, a sense of community in the village is deliberately encouraged through the organisation of group activities.

You may wonder how we ended up living in Brassington village. Why did we want to live in a village, especially one with so few amenities? And why in Derbyshire? We had spent the last eight years living in China, where John worked at the overseas campus of the University of Nottingham in Ningbo. We had all along expected that this would be John's last job and we would both retire when we were ready. We were looking forward to it. When we first started discussing our retirement, we did not automatically assume we would retire to England, and we considered a few other European countries, the Netherlands in particular. Brexit put an end to that! So, we had to start considering where in England we might want to live. There were plenty of things to take into consideration. The first of these was that, having lived away from our children and grandchildren for the previous eight years, we wanted somewhere within easy travelling distance of all of them. Our younger daughter, Farida, and her family were living in Dubai and looked likely to stay there for a long time, so being close to them was not an option. On the other hand though, at least we have an escape option, somewhere warm and welcoming to visit in the middle of a cold English winter.

John wanted us to look for somewhere with easy access to 'good' walks, by which he meant somewhere with nearby hills! He wanted somewhere where we could go for interesting walks straight from the door of our house. This would probably mean living in a village or at most a small town. John is not a city person, and eight years of living in a large Chinese city was enough to confirm it for him. I wasn't quite as keen on living somewhere "remote," perhaps because of my experience of village life in Africa. I wanted a modern house, access to shops, and lots of people around. However, I have never regretted coming to live in Brassington village, and I love it here. But I still enjoy walking — around the shops — and sitting with a coffee with people all around me, so I enjoy frequent trips to Matlock, Ashbourne and Bakewell – not big cities but a welcome change when I am feeling a bit isolated.

Our daughter, Tuni, started looking for a house for us before John completed his contract, and we cannot thank her enough for finding the place we now call home. She looked for somewhere in Derbyshire because we had mentioned it to all our children as a place we would like to retire in. John's mother had family roots in Derbyshire and grew up in Chesterfield, and John had happy childhood memories of visiting his aunt there. We always came to England from China in summer, and visited Derbyshire, which always seemed to give us sunshine and blue skies, as well as beautiful hills and dales. Perhaps we naively assumed that our life in retirement would be all sunshine and walks.

Tuni found this beautiful cottage in Brassington, a village that we knew nothing about at that time although she told us later that she had been there during a family holiday. We liked the agent's photos and videos, which we looked at on the Internet. I think it was the garden that really won me over at that time. The garden was on the side of a hill and full of flowers and trees, with Derbyshire stone walls marking out the different sections. When we went to view the cottage, however, it was the view from the garden that struck me most — down the sloping valley where the village lies, and then beyond, to distant hills and woods. It also helped that we came to see it on a sunny day, reinforcing my impression that Derbyshire is always sunny! The views from the cottage looking over to the surrounding hills also reminded me of my birth village of Usangi.

Unsurprisingly, we weren't the only potential buyers tempted by the charm of this traditional stone cottage and its views. Tuni and I went to look it over during the Covid pandemic, when the number of visitors at any one time was limited to just two. The day we came to view the cottage we were immediately bowled over, struck by the beauty of the views. Even if you manage to find the village of Brassington, the cottage itself is located on the side of a steep hill and is accessed by a narrow road with two sharp bends and stone walls on either side. At that time we did not appreciate the significance of this but we have since learned — and learned to laugh about — the consequences in terms of parking and guiding visitors to our address.

That day we first came to view the cottage, we carefully tucked our car into the roadside opposite and were told to wait in the garden, as there were already two people inside the house. This, fortunately, gave us a great opportunity to explore the garden and take in the views. I think that if we had been asked to make an offer for the house right there and then, before we had even been inside, we would probably have said "Yes!" I already knew at that point that this was the house we had been looking for. But it wasn't going to be quite as easy as that. I had never before been inside a "traditional" English cottage, and I was struck by how small the rooms were and how low the ceiling was. The saving features for me were a wonderfully light and airy new extension that would become our main living area, and a separate wooden building which we now call the "summer house." Perhaps if it had been one of the wet and misty days that we have experienced since then, or if the garden had not offered such delightful treasures, we might have had second thoughts. Now I think, "Thank goodness it wasn't that sort of a day!" You could say it was the sunshine that decided for us, and I have never regretted it.

Later on the same day, Tuni rang the agency and put in our offer. We were too late. The couple who had been just ahead of us had beaten us to it. They had made an offer that had been accepted. It really was a bad moment for us after we had allowed ourselves to be so enthusiastic about the cottage. John was at that time stranded in China by the COVID-19 restrictions on travel. He too had been so excited about it from the pictures we had sent him, and had to deal with the disappointment on his own. We had no choice but to start looking again but somehow nothing seemed to match up to Jackdaw Cottage. We struggled to raise any enthusiasm about the other houses we found. There was always something wrong with each one of them — the location, the garden, the views…

But there was to be yet another twist to the story. Maybe someone was looking over us — or playing games with us — because, some months later, when I was back in China, the agent informed us that the people whose offer had been accepted had decided to pull out. Were we still interested? Were we? No, we were not interested … we were thrilled, overjoyed, and could hardly believe our luck! At the time we had two months to go before John's contract finished, so all the business of buying the property had to be done at a distance. We frantically tried to get everything done in time, so that we could move in as soon as we got back to England, while also finishing up in China (which is a whole other story). If you have never tried buying a house from half a world away, don't. It was a nightmare. But once all the documents were signed and delivered, John and I finally allowed ourselves a big sigh of relief. We now had a home to go to when John's contract ended. As much by luck as by planning, everything turned out to have been well timed!

John and I feel we have settled very well in Brassington. I was delighted and proud when I was invited to join the over-sixties group. It meant I had been accepted as a member of the village community. The group organises meetings and activities, but is mostly just a great opportunity for getting together for a chat. We do this once a month, and everyone is welcome to give a talk or presentation to the other members of the group. It is fascinating to discover the range of different backgrounds, lives and activities there is in this small, quiet village. We are not at all shut off from the world; we, the inhabitants, bring the world into the village. I have given several talks about my earlier life and African culture. A younger resident of the village has shared his experiences of living and working in the Antarctic; another lady talked about her experiences of Rwanda; and of course there is a wealth of knowledge about Derbyshire, from walking routes to dialects. It is also our way of keeping us united as villagers, maintaining contact and caring for our neighbours. If someone who usually attends does not turn up for a couple of meetings, the rest of us are concerned and try to find out if there is anything wrong or anything we can do to help. Meetings of the over-sixties are something I now look forward to, both for the pleasure of the meeting but also for feeling it gives me that I 'belong' here.

I have also joined another group which meets every Wednesday morning in the British Legion Hall, purely for a chat, along with tea and toast. We invite anyone who might be interested to join us, whether residents or not, including passers-by and walkers - with dogs or without. If you ever happen to be in Brassington on a Wednesday morning, please do drop in.

I would like to finish this chapter by saying that, despite all the differences among the many cultures I have experienced, I still believe that we have more in common than we have differences between us. We all want much the same. We all want to be loved and respected, whatever colour we are, or wherever we come from. I have learned that we can learn to live together if we want to, and if we are prepared to make an effort to accept each other. We should not only accept but also welcome the differences between us that actually make the world so much more interesting. Certainly I believe that the world can be a better place for us all to live in if we really want it to be.

Acknowledgments

I would like to thank my husband John and our four children Tuni, Mani, Farida and Nurudin, who have supported and encouraged me, not only in writing but in so much more and I am very proud of you all and I love you. John, you have changed my life for the better. The best thing I ever did was to marry you. You are everything I could possibly have asked for and you have a special place in my heart. You are my life, my hero, my world and I wouldn't change you for anyone. I thank you not only for what you did for me, but what you also did for my African family through your generous gestures and financial support – and so much more besides. You have touched many people's lives, not only my own, and I love you.

I would also like to give a special thank you to Anne, who is one of our best friends and also my editor, and who has proofread and edited this book. Thank you Anne. I would also like to say a big thank you to my families in Kenya and Tanzania, who have always made me welcome in their homes. Your love and warm smiles will always be remembered.

I would like to say that John and I are very proud to have brought up four children who have all done well in their lives. Tuni, Mani and Farida have between them given us eight grandchildren whom we love dearly.

About the Author

Aisha Lowe was born in 1957 in a rural village in what was then known as Tanganyika. She came to England with her husband and four children in 1984. Three years later, the family went to live in the Solomon Islands, staying there for six years before returning to England, where Aisha went on to work in a variety of jobs. Later she and her husband spent eight years in China before retiring to live in Derbyshire village, where they enjoy walking, gardening, travelling and visiting their children and grandchildren in England and Dubai. In her retirement Aisha has also developed an enthusiasm for table tennis – when she is not writing.